MONOLINGUAL

OXFORD PICTURE DICTIONARY

SECOND EDITION

Jayme Adelson-Goldstein

Norma Shapiro

OXFORD
UNIVERSITY PRESS

198 Madison Avenue
New York, NY 10016 USA

Great Clarendon Street, Oxford OX2 6DP UK

Oxford University Press is a department of the University of Oxford.
It furthers the University's objective of excellence in research, scholarship,
and education by publishing worldwide in

Oxford New York

Auckland Cape Town Dar es Salaam Hong Kong Karachi
Kuala Lumpur Madrid Melbourne Mexico City Nairobi
New Delhi Shanghai Taipei Toronto

With offices in

Argentina Austria Brazil Chile Czech Republic France Greece
Guatemala Hungary Italy Japan Poland Portugal Singapore
South Korea Switzerland Thailand Turkey Ukraine Vietnam

OXFORD and OXFORD ENGLISH are registered trademarks of
Oxford University Press.

© Oxford University Press 2008

Library of Congress Cataloging-in-Publication Data

Adelson-Goldstein, Jayme.
    The Oxford picture dictionary. Monolingual /
Jayme Adelson-Goldstein and Norma Shapiro.– 2nd ed.
        p. cm.
    Includes index.
    ISBN: 978-0-19-436976-3

    1. Picture dictionaries, English. 2. English
language--Textbooks for foreign speakers.
I. Shapiro, Norma. II. Title.
PE1629.S52 2008
423'.1–dc22

                                        2007041017

Database right Oxford University Press (maker)

Executive Publishing Manager: Stephanie Karras
Managing Editor: Sharon Sargent
Development Editors: Glenn Mathes II, Bruce Myint, Katie La Storia
Associate Development Editors: Olga Christopoulos, Hannah Ryu
Design Manager: Maj-Britt Hagsted
Project Manager: Allison Harm
Senior Designers: Stacy Merlin, Michael Steinhofer
Designer: Jaclyn Smith
Senior Production Artist: Julie Armstrong
Production Layout Artist: Colleen Ho
Cover Design: Stacy Merlin
Senior Image Editor: Justine Eun
Image Editors: Robin Fadool, Fran Newman, Jenny Vainisi
Manufacturing Manager: Shanta Persaud
Manufacturing Controller: Eve Wong

ISBN: 978 0 19 436976 3

Printed in China

10 9 8 7 6

This book is printed on paper from certified and well-managed sources.

The OPD team thanks the following artists for their storyboarding and sketches:
Cecilia Aranovich, Chris Brandt, Giacomo Ghiazza, Gary Goldstein, Gordan Kljucec,
Vincent Lucido, and Glenn Urieta

Illustrations by: Lori Anzalone: 13, 70-71, 76-77; Joe "Fearless" Arenella/Will Sumpter:
178; Argosy Publishing: 66-67 (call-outs), 98-99, 108-109, 112-113 (call-outs), 152, 178,
193, 194-195, 196, 197, 205; Barbara Bastian: 4, 15, 17, 20-21, 162 (map), 198, 216-217
(map), 220-221; Philip Batini/AA Reps: 50; Thomas Bayley/Sparks Literary Agency:
158-159; Sally Bensusen: 211, 214; Annie Bissett: 112; Peter Bollinger/Shannon
Associates: 14-15; Higgens Bond/Anita Grien: 226; Molly Borman-Pullman: 116,
117; Jim Fanning/Ravenhill Represents: 80-81; Mike Gardner: 10, 12, 17, 22, 132,
114-115, 142-143, 174, 219, 228-229; Garth Glazier/AA Reps: 106, 118-119; Dennis
Godfrey/Mike Wepplo: 204; Steve Graham: 124-125, 224; Graphic Map & Chart Co.:
200-201, 202-203; Julia Green/Mendola Art: 225; Glenn Gustafson: 9, 27, 48, 76,
100, 101, 117, 132, 133, 136, 155, 161, 179, 196; Barbara Harmon: 212-213, 215; Ben
Hasler/NB Illustration: 94-95, 101, 148-149, 172, 182, 186-187; Betsy Hayes: 134,
138-139; Matthew Holmes: 75; Stewart Holmes/Illustration Ltd.: 192; Janos Jantner/
Beehive Illustration: 5, 13, 82-83, 122-123, 130-131, 146-147, 164-165, 184, 185; Ken
Joudrey/Munro Campagna: 52, 68-69, 177, 208-209; Bob Kaganich/Deborah Wolfe:
10, 40-41, 121; Steve Karp: 230, 231; Mike Kasun/Munro Campagna: 218; Graham
Kennedy: 27; Marcel Laverdet/AA Reps: 23; Jeffrey Lindberg: 33, 42-43, 92-93, 133,
160-161, 170-171, 176; Dennis Lyall/Artworks: 198; Chris Lyons:/Lindgren & Smith:
173, 191; Alan Male/Artworks: 210, 211; Jeff Mangiat/Mendola Art: 53, 54, 55, 56, 57,
58, 59, 66-67; Adrian Mateescu/The Studio: 188-189, 232-233; Karen Minot: 28-29;
Paul Mirocha/The Wiley Group: 194, 216-217; Peter Miserendino/P.T. Pie Illustrations:
198; Lee Montgomery/Illustration Ltd.: 4; Roger Motzkus: 229; Laurie O'Keefe: 111,
216-217; Daniel O'Leary/Illustration Ltd.: 8-9, 26, 34-35, 78, 135, 136-137, 238; Vilma
Ortiz-Dillon: 16, 20-21, 60, 98-99, 100, 211; Terry Pazcko: 46-47, 144-145, 152, 180,
227; David Preiss/Munro Campagna: 5; Pronk & Associates: 192-193; Tony Randazzo/
AA Reps: 156, 234-235; Mike Renwick/Creative Eye: 126-127; Mark Riedy/Scott Hull
Associates: 48-49, 79, 140, 153; Jon Rogers/AA Reps: 112; Jeff Sanson/Schumann &
Co.: 84-85, 240-241; David Schweitzer/Munro Campagna: 162-163; Ben Shannon/
Magnet Reps: 11, 64-65, 90, 91, 96, 97, 166-167, 168-169, 179, 239; Reed Sprunger/
Jae Wagoner Artists Rep.: 18-19, 232-233; Studio Liddell/AA Reps: 27; Angelo Tillary:
108-109; Ralph Voltz/Deborah Wolfe: 50-51, 128-129, 141, 154, 175, 236-237;
Jeff Wack/Mendola Art: 24, 25, 86-87, 102-103, 134-135, 231; Brad Walker: 104-105,
150-151, 157, 206-207; Wendy Wassink: 110-111; John White/The Neis Group: 199;
Eric Wilkerson: 32, 138; Simon Williams/Illustration Ltd.: 2-3, 6-7, 30-31, 36, 38-39,
44-45, 72-73; Lee Woodgate/Eye Candy Illustration: 222-223; Andy Zito: 62-23; Craig
Zuckerman: 14, 88-89, 112-113, 120-121, 194-195.

Chapter icons designed by Von Glitschka/Scott Hull Associates

Cover Art by CUBE/Illustration Ltd (hummingbird, branch); Paul Mirocha/The Wiley
Group (cherry); Mark Riedy/Scott Hull Associates (stamp); 9 Surf Studios (lettering).

Studio photography for Oxford University Press done by Dennis Kitchen Studio: 37,
61, 72, 73, 74, 75, 95, 96, 100, 180, 181, 183, 226.

Stock Photography: Age FotoStock: 238 (flute; clarinet; bassoon; saxophone; violin; cello;
bass; guitar; trombone; trumpet; xylophone; harmonica); Comstock, 61 (window);
Morales, 221 (bat); Franco Pizzochero, 98 (cashmere); Thinkstock, 61 (sink); Alamy:
Corbis, 61 (table); Gary Crabbe, 220 (park ranger); The Associated Press: 198 (strike;
soldiers in trench); Joe Rosenthal, 198 (Iwo Jima); Neil Armstrong, 198 (Buzz Aldrin
on Moon); CORBIS: Philip Gould, 198 (Civil War); Photo Library, 220 (Yosemite Falls);
Danita Delimont: Greg Johnston, 220 (snorkeling); Jamie & Judy Wild, 220 (El Capitan);
Getty Images: 198 (Martin Luther King, Jr.); Amana Images, 61 (soapy plates), The
Granger Collection: 198 (Jazz Age); The Image Works: Kelly Spranger, 220 (sea turtle);
Inmagine: 238 (oboe; tuba; French horn; piano; drums; tambourine; accordion);
istockphoto: 61 (oven), 98 (silk), 99 (suede; lace; velvet); Jupiter Images: 61 (tiles); 98
(wool); 99 (corduroy); Foodpix, 98 (linen); Rob Melnychuk/Brand X Pictures: 61 (glass
shower door); Jupiter Unlimited: 220 (seagulls); 238 (electric keyboard); Comstock, 99
(denim); Mary Evans Picture Library: 198 (women in factory); NPS Photo: Peter Jones, 221
(Carlsbad Cavern entrance; tour; cavern; spelunker); OceanwideImages.com: Gary Bell,
220 (coral); Photo Edit, Inc: David Young-Wolff, 220 (trail); Picture History: 198 (Hiram
Rhodes); Robertstock: 198 (Great Depression); Punchstock: 98 (t-shirt), Robert Glusic,
31 (Monument Valley); Roland Corporation: 238 (organ); SuperStock: 99 (leather); 198
(Daniel Boone); Shutterstock: Marek Szumlas, 94 (watch); United States Mint: 126;
Veer: Brand X Pictures, 220 (deer); Photodisc, 220 (black bear); Yankee Fleet, Inc.: 220
(Fort Jefferson; Yankee Freedom Ferry), Emil von Maltitz/Lime Photo, 37 (baby carrier).

This second edition of
the Oxford Picture Dictionary
is lovingly dedicated to
the memory of Norma Shapiro.

Her ideas, her pictures, and
her stories continue to teach,
inspire, and delight.

Acknowledgments

The publisher and authors would like to acknowledge the following individuals for their invaluable feedback during the development of this program:

Dr. Macarena Aguilar, Cy-Fair College, Houston, TX

Joseph F. Anselme, Atlantic Technical Center, Coconut Creek, FL

Stacy Antonopoulos, Monterey Trail High School, Elk Grove, CA

Carol Antunano, The English Center, Miami, FL

Irma Arencibia, Thomas A. Edison School, Union City, NJ

Suzi Austin, Alexandria City Public School Adult Program, Alexandria, FL

Patricia S. Bell, Lake Technical Center, Eustis, FL

Jim Brice, San Diego Community College District, San Diego, CA

Phil Cackley, Arlington Education and Employment Program (REEP), Arlington, VA

Frieda Caldwell, Metropolitan Adult Education Program, San Jose, CA

Sandra Cancel, Robert Waters School, Union City, NJ

Anne Marie Caney, Chula Vista Adult School, Chula Vista, CA

Patricia Castro, Harvest English Institute, Newark, NJ

Paohui Lola Chen, Milpitas Adult School, Milpitas, CA

Lori Cisneros, Atlantic Vo-Tech, Ft. Lauderdale, FL

Joyce Clapp, Hayward Adult School, Hayward, CA

Stacy Clark, Arlington Education and Employment Program (REEP), Arlington, VA

Nancy B. Crowell, Southside Programs for Adults in Continuing Education, Prince George, VA

Doroti da Cunha, Hialeah-Miami Lakes Adult Education Center, Miami, FL

Paula Da Silva-Michelin, La Guardia Community College, Long Island City, NY

Cynthia L. Davies, Humble I.S.D., Humble, TX

Christopher Davis, Overfelt Adult Center, San Jose, CA

Beverly De Nicola, Capistrano Unified School District, San Juan Capistrano, CA

Beatriz Diaz, Miami-Dade County Public Schools, Miami, FL

Druci J. Diaz, Hillsborough County Public Schools, Tampa, FL

Marion Donahue, San Dieguito Adult School, Encinitas, CA

Nick Doorn, International Education Services, South Lyon, MI

Mercedes Douglass, Seminole Community College, Sanford, FL

Jenny Elliott, Montgomery College, Rockville, MD

Paige Endo, Mt. Diablo Adult Education, Concord, CA

Megan Ernst, Glendale Community College, Glendale, CA

Elizabeth Escobar, Robert Waters School, Union City, NJ

Joanne Everett, Dave Thomas Education Center, Pompano Beach, FL

Jennifer Fadden, Arlington Education and Employment Program (REEP), Arlington, VA

Judy Farron, Fort Myers Language Center, Fort Myers, FL

Sharyl Ferguson, Montwood High School, El Paso, TX

Dr. Monica Fishkin, University of Central Florida, Orlando, FL

Nancy Frampton, Reedley College, Reedley, CA

Lynn A. Freeland, San Dieguito Union High School District, Encinitas, CA

Cathy Gample, San Leandro Adult School, San Leandro, CA

Hillary Gardner, Center for Immigrant Education and Training, Long Island City, NY

Martha C. Giffen, Alhambra Unified School District, Alhambra, CA

Jill Gluck, Hollywood Community Adult School, Los Angeles, CA

Carolyn Grimaldi, LaGuardia Community College, Long Island City, NY

William Gruenholz, USD Adult School, Concord, CA

Sandra G. Gutierrez, Hialeah-Miami Lakes Adult Education Center, Miami, FL

Conte Gúzman-Hoffman, Triton College, River Grove, IL

Amanda Harllee, Palmetto High School, Palmetto, FL

Mercedes Hearn, Tampa Bay Technical Center, Tampa, FL

Robert Hearst, Truman College, Chicago, IL

Patty Heiser, University of Washington, Seattle, WA

Joyce Hettiger, Metropolitan Education District, San Jose, CA

Karen Hirsimaki, Napa Valley Adult School, Napa, CA

Marvina Hooper, Lake Technical Center, Eustis, FL

Katie Hurter, North Harris College, Houston, TX

Nuchamon James, Miami Dade College, Miami, FL

Linda Jennings, Montgomery College, Rockville, MD

Bonnie Boyd Johnson, Chapman Education Center, Garden Grove, CA

Fayne B. Johnson, Broward County Public Schools, Fort Lauderdale, FL

Stavroula Katseyeanis, Robert Waters School, Union City, NJ

Dale Keith, Broadbase Consulting, Inc. at Kidworks USA, Miami, FL

Blanche Kellawon, Bronx Community College, Bronx, NY

Mary Kernel, Migrant Education Regional Office, Northwest Educational Service District, Anacortes, WA

Karen Kipke, Antioch High School Freshman Academy, Antioch, TN

Jody Kirkwood, ABC Adult School, Cerritos, CA

Matthew Kogan, Evans Community Adult School, Los Angeles, CA

Ineza Kuceba, Renton Technical College, Renton, WA

John Kuntz, California State University, San Bernadino, San Bernadino, CA

Claudia Kupiec, DePaul University, Chicago, IL

E.C. Land, Southside Programs for Adult Continuing Education, Prince George, VA

Betty Lau, Franklin High School, Seattle, WA

Patt Lemonie, Thomas A. Edison School, Union City, NJ

Lia Lerner, Burbank Adult School, Burbank, CA

Krystyna Lett, Metropolitan Education District, San Jose, CA

Renata Lima, TALK International School of Languages, Fort Lauderdale, FL

Luz M. Lopez, Sweetwater Union High School District, Chula Vista, CA

Osmara Lopez, Bronx Community College, Bronx, NY

Heather Lozano, North Lake College, Irving, TX

Betty Lynch, Arlington Education and Employment Program (REEP), Arlington, VA

Meera Madan, REID Park Elementary School, Charlotte, NC

Ivanna Mann Thrower, Charlotte Mecklenburg Schools, Charlotte, NC

Michael R. Mason, Loma Vista Adult Center, Concord, CA

Holley Mayville, Charlotte Mecklenburg Schools, Charlotte, NC

Margaret McCabe, United Methodist Cooperative Ministries, Clearwater, FL

Todd McDonald, Hillsborough Adult Education, Tampa, FL

Nancy A. McKeand, ESL Consultant, St. Benedict, LA

Rebecca L. McLain, Gaston College, Dallas, NC

John M. Mendoza, Redlands Adult School, Redlands, CA

Bet Messmer, Santa Clara Adult Education Center, Santa Clara, CA

Christina Morales, BEGIN Managed Programs, New York, NY

Lisa Munoz, Metropolitan Education District, San Jose, CA

Mary Murphy-Clagett, Sweetwater Union High School District, Chula Vista, CA

Jonetta Myles, Rockdale County High School, Conyers, GA

Marwan Nabi, Troy High School, Fullerton, CA

Dr. Christine L. Nelsen, Salvation Army Community Center, Tampa, FL

Michael W. Newman, Arlington Education and Employment Program (REEP), Arlington, VA

Rehana Nusrat, Huntington Beach Adult School, Huntington Beach, CA

Cindy Oakley-Paulik, Embry-Riddle Aeronautical University, Daytona Beach, FL

Acknowledgments

Janet Ochi-Fontanott, Sweetwater Union High School District, Chula Vista, CA

Lorraine Pedretti, Metropolitan Education District, San Jose, CA

Isabel Pena, BE/ESL Programs, Garland, TX

Margaret Perry, Everett Public Schools, Everett, WA

Dale Pesmen, PhD, Chicago, IL

Cathleen Petersen, Chapman Education Center, Garden Grove, CA

Allison Pickering, Escondido Adult School, Escondido, CA

Ellen Quish, LaGuardia Community College, Long Island City, NY

Teresa Reen, Independence Adult Center, San Jose, CA

Kathleen Reynolds, Albany Park Community Center, Chicago, IL

Melba I. Rillen, Palmetto High School, Palmetto, FL

Lorraine Romero, Houston Community College, Houston, TX

Eric Rosenbaum, BEGIN Managed Programs, New York, NY

Blair Roy, Chapman Education Center, Garden Grove, CA

Arlene R. Schwartz, Broward Community Schools, Fort Lauderdale, FL

Geraldyne Blake Scott, Truman College, Chicago, IL

Sharada Sekar, Antioch High School Freshman Academy, Antioch, TN

Dr. Cheryl J. Serrano, Lynn University, Boca Raton, FL

Janet Setzekorn, United Methodist Cooperative Ministries, Clearwater, FL

Terry Shearer, EDUCALL Learning Services, Houston, TX

Elisabeth Sklar, Township High School District 113, Highland Park, IL

Robert Stein, BEGIN Managed Programs, New York, NY

Ruth Sutton, Township High School District 113, Highland Park, IL

Alisa Takeuchi, Chapman Education Center, Garden Grove, CA

Grace Tanaka, Santa Ana College School of Continuing Education, Santa Ana, CA

Annalisa Te, Overfelt Adult Center, San Jose, CA

Don Torluemke, South Bay Adult School, Redondo Beach, CA

Maliheh Vafai, Overfelt Adult Center, San Jose, CA

Tara Vasquez, Robert Waters School, Union City, NJ

Nina Velasco, Naples Language Center, Naples, FL

Theresa Warren, East Side Adult Center, San Jose, CA

Lucie Gates Watel, Truman College, Chicago, IL

Wendy Weil, Arnold Middle School, Cypress, TX

Patricia Weist, TALK International School of Languages, Fort Lauderdale, FL

Dr. Carole Lynn Weisz, Lehman College, Bronx, NY

Desiree Wesner, Robert Waters School, Union City, NJ

David Wexler, Napa Valley Adult School, Napa, CA

Cynthia Wiseman, Borough of Manhattan Community College, New York, NY

Debbie Cullinane Wood, Lincoln Education Center, Garden Grove, CA

Banu Yaylali, Miami Dade College, Miami, FL

Hongyan Zheng, Milpitas Adult Education, Milpitas, CA

Arlene Zivitz, ESOL Teacher, Jupiter, FL

The publisher, authors, and editors would like to thank the following people for their expertise in reviewing specific content areas:

Ross Feldberg, Tufts University, Medford, MA

William J. Hall, M.D. FACP/FRSM (UK), Cumberland Foreside, ME

Jill A. Horohoe, Arizona State University, Tempe, AZ

Phoebe B. Rouse, Louisiana State University, Baton Rouge, LA

Dr. Susan Rouse, Southern Wesleyan University, Central, SC

Dr. Ira M. Sheskin, University of Miami, Coral Gables, FL

Maiko Tomizawa, D.D.S., New York, NY

The author lovingly acknowledges the extraordinary people at Oxford who worked so tirelessly to make OPD 2e an OPD for the 21st century. Special thanks to Stephanie—for her vision and verve; Glenn—for his brilliant ideas and constant support; Bruce—for his unerring eye and rapier wit; Katie—for always getting to the heart of the issue; Sharon—for her ability to make the impossible possible; Maj—for "getting OPD" so completely; Stacy, Michael and Claudia—for their absolutely wonderful sense of design; Fran, Justine, Robin and Jenni—for their artistic understanding; Myndee, Joe, Laura and Margaret—for believing in a second edition; and Shanta and Eve—for making sure that edition got into print.

There are many other people who stood beside me during this project. I humbly thank Gordan, Chris, Vincent, Glenn, Cecilia and my own Gary for sketching out each page of the book with me. I am indebted to Jane, Jenni, Marjorie and Margot for the time they spent reviewing word lists and art while working on their own books. Norma, of course, made her presence known many times. (See page 169.) I am also grateful to Karen Clark and my own Emily. Without their organizational skills, I would still be drowning in reams and reams of art and words.

And last, but certainly not least, I thank all the students and teachers I've worked with over the past 25 years. Your input is on every page.

xo j/me

Table of Contents

Contents

4. Food

5. Clothing

6. Health

7. Community

8. Transportation

9. Work

Contents

Teaching with the *Oxford Picture Dictionary* Program

The following general guidelines will help you prepare single and multilevel lessons using the OPD program. For step-by-step, topic-specific lesson plans, see *OPD Lesson Plans*.

1. Use Students' Needs to Identify Lesson Objectives

- Create communicative objectives based on your learners' needs assessments (*see OPD 2e Assessment Program*).
- Make sure objectives state what students will be able to do at the end of the lesson. For example: *Students will be able to respond to basic classroom commands and requests for classroom objects.* (pp. 6–7, A Classroom)
- For multilevel classes, identify a low-beginning, high-beginning, and low-intermediate objective for each topic.

2. Preview the Topic

Identify what your students already know about the topic.

- Ask general questions related to the topic.
- Have students list words they know from the topic.
- Ask questions about the picture(s) on the page.

3. Present the New Vocabulary

Research shows that it is best to present no more than 5–7 new words at a time. Here are a few presentation techniques:

- Say each new word and describe it within the context of the picture. Have volunteers act out verbs and verb sequences.
- Use Total Physical Response commands to build vocabulary comprehension.
- For long or unfamiliar word lists, introduce words by categories or select the words your students need most.
- Ask a series of questions to build comprehension and give students an opportunity to say the new words. Begin with *yes/no* questions: *Is #16 chalk?* Progress to *or* questions: *Is #16 chalk or a marker?* Finally, ask *Wh-* questions: *What can I use to write on this paper?*
- Focus on the words that students want to learn. Have them write 3–5 new words from each topic, along with meaning clues such as a drawing, translation, or sentence.

More vocabulary and **Grammar Point** sections provide additional presentation opportunities (see p. 5, School). For multilevel presentation ideas, see *OPD Lesson Plans*.

4. Check Comprehension

Make sure that students understand the target vocabulary. Here are two activities you can try:

- Say vocabulary words, and have students point to the correct items in their books. Walk around the room, checking if students are pointing to the correct pictures.
- Make true/false statements about the target vocabulary. Have students hold up two fingers for true, three for false.

5. Provide Guided and Communicative Practice

The exercise bands at the bottom of the topic pages provide a variety of guided and communicative practice opportunities and engage students' higher-level thinking.

6. Provide More Practice

OPD Second Edition offers a variety of components to facilitate vocabulary acquisition. Each of the print and electronic materials listed below offers suggestions and support for single and multilevel instruction.

OPD Lesson Plans Step-by-step multilevel lesson plans feature 3 CDs with multilevel listening, context-based pronunciation practice, and leveled reading practice. Includes multilevel teaching notes for *The OPD Reading Library*.

OPD Audio CDs or Audio Cassettes Each word in *OPD's* word list is recorded by topic.

Low-Beginning, High-Beginning, and Low-Intermediate Workbooks Guided practice for each page in *OPD* features linked visual contexts, realia, and listening practice.

Classic Classroom Activities A photocopiable resource of interactive multilevel activities, grammar practice, and communicative tasks.

The OPD Reading Library Readers include civics, academic content, and workplace themes.

Overhead Transparencies Vibrant transparencies help to focus students on the lesson.

OPD Presentation Software A multilevel interactive teaching tool using interactive whiteboard and LCD technology. Audio, animation, and video instructional support bring each dictionary topic to life.

The OPD CD-ROM An interactive learning tool featuring four-skill practice based on *OPD* topics.

Bilingual Editions *OPD* is available in numerous bilingual editions including Spanish, Chinese, Vietnamese, Arabic, Korean, and many more.

My hope is that OPD makes it easier for you to take your learners from comprehension to communication. Please share your thoughts with us as you make the book your own.

Jayme Adelson-Goldstein

Jayme Adelson-Goldstein

OPDteam.us@oup.com

Welcome to the
OPD SECOND EDITION

The second edition of the *Oxford Picture Dictionary* expands on the best aspects of the 1998 edition with:

- New artwork presenting words within meaningful, real-life contexts
- An updated word list to meet the needs of today's English language learners
- 4,000 English words and phrases, including 285 verbs
- 40 new topics with 12 intro pages and 12 story pages
- Unparalleled support for vocabulary teaching

Subtopics present the words in easy-to-learn "chunks."

Color coding and icons make it easy to navigate through *OPD*.

New art and rich contexts improve vocabulary acquisition.

Public Transportation

A Bus Stop

BUS 10 Northbound		
Main	Elm	Oak
6:00	6:10	6:13
6:30	6:40	6:43
7:00	7:10	7:13
7:30	7:40	7:43

Transfer

A Subway Station

MetroCard

1. bus route	3. rider	5. transfer
2. fare	4. schedule	

6. subway car	8. turnstile	10. token
7. platform	9. vending machine	11. fare card

A Train Station

HART DAVIS/DAMON
DOVER, NH
BOSTON NRTH STA,MA
2V 684 17FEB03
2V BUSINESS CL
AP XXXXX0456791 Ax

Fresno — Los Angeles
Fresno — Los Angeles

Airport Transportation

12. ticket window	15. ticket	18. taxi stand	21. taxi driver
13. conductor	16. one-way trip	19. shuttle	22. taxi license
14. track	17. round trip	20. town car	23. meter

More vocabulary	Ask your classmates. Share the answers.
hail a taxi: to raise your hand to get a taxi	1. Is there a subway system in your city?
miss the bus: to get to the bus stop after the bus leaves	2. Do you ever take taxis? When?
	3. Do you ever take the bus? Where?

152

Revised practice activities help students from low-beginning through low-intermediate levels.

NEW! Intro pages open each unit with key vocabulary related to the unit theme. Clear, engaging artwork promotes questions, conversations, and writing practice for all levels.

Each intro page teaches key vocabulary items within the unit theme.

Practice activities make it easy to manage multilevel classrooms.

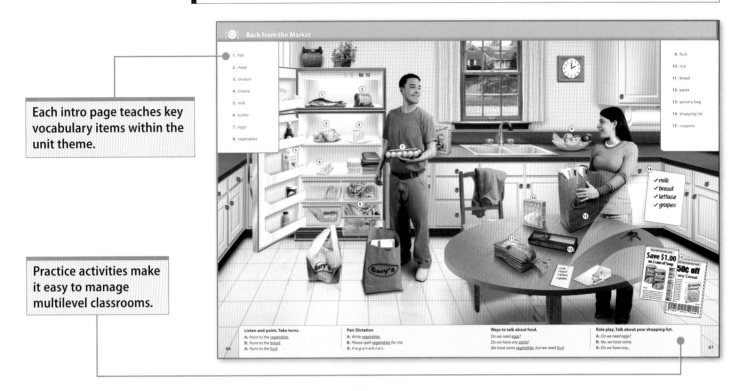

NEW! Story pages close each unit with a lively scene for reviewing vocabulary and teaching additional language. Meanwhile, rich visual contexts recycle words from the unit.

Pre-reading questions build students' previewing and predicting skills.

High-interest readings promote literacy skills.

Post-reading questions and role-play activities support critical thinking and encourage students to use the language they have learned.

The thematic word list previews words that students will encounter in the story.

Meeting and Greeting

A. **Say**, "Hello."

B. **Ask**, "How are you?"

C. **Introduce** yourself.

D. **Smile**.

E. **Hug**.

F. **Wave**.

Tell your partner what to do. Take turns.

1. *Say,* "Hello."   4. *Shake hands.*
2. *Bow.*   5. *Wave.*
3. *Smile.*   6. *Say,* "Goodbye."

Dictate to your partner. Take turns.

A: *Write* <u>smile</u>.
B: *Is it spelled* <u>s-m-i-l-e</u>?
A: *Yes, that's right.*

2

G. **Greet** people.

H. **Bow**.

I. **Introduce** a friend.

J. **Shake** hands.

K. **Kiss**.

L. **Say**, "Goodbye."

Ways to greet people

Good morning.
Good afternoon.
Good evening.

Ways to introduce yourself

I'm Tom.
My name is Tom.

Pair practice. Make new conversations.

A: *Good morning. My name is Tom.*
B: *Nice to meet you, Tom. I'm Sara.*
A: *Nice to meet you, Sara.*

A. **Say** your name.

B. **Spell** your name.

C. **Print** your name.

D. **Sign** your name.

Filling Out a Form

School Registration Form

1. name:

_____ _____ _____ _____ _____

2. first name **3.** middle initial **4.** last name **5.** address **6.** apartment number

_____ _____ _____ (   )_____ _____

7. city **8.** state **9.** ZIP code **10.** area code **11.** phone number

(   )_____ _____ _____

12. cell phone number **13.** date of birth (DOB) **14.** place of birth

_____ - ____ - _____   **16.** sex: **17.** male ☐ _____

15. Social Security number   **18.** female ☐ **19.** signature

---

Pair practice. Make new conversations.

A: *My first name is Carlos.*
B: *Please spell Carlos for me.*
A: *C-a-r-l-o-s*

Ask your classmates. Share the answers.

1. Do you like your first name?
2. Is your last name from your mother? father? husband?
3. What is your middle name?

Campus

1. quad
2. field
3. bleachers
4. principal
5. assistant principal
6. counselor
7. classroom
8. teacher
9. restrooms
10. hallway
11. locker
12. main office
13. clerk
14. cafeteria
15. computer lab
16. teacher's aide
17. library
18. auditorium
19. gym
20. coach
21. track

Administrators

Around Campus

More vocabulary

Students do not pay to go to a **public school**.
Students pay to go to a **private school**.
A church, mosque, or temple school is a **parochial school**.

Grammar Point: contractions of the verb *be*

He + is = He's   *He's a teacher.*
She + is = She's   *She's a counselor.*
They + are = They're   *They're students.*

5

1. chalkboard
2. screen
3. whiteboard
4. teacher / instructor
5. student
6. LCD projector
7. desk
8. headphones

A. **Raise** your hand.

B. **Talk** to the teacher.

C. **Listen** to a CD.

D. **Stand up**.

E. **Write** on the board.

F. **Sit down**. / **Take** a seat.

G. **Open** your book.

H. **Close** your book.

I. **Pick up** the pencil.

J. **Put down** the pencil.

ABCDEFGHIJKLMNOPQRSTUVWXYZ

9. clock

10. bookcase

11. chair

12. map

13. alphabet

14. bulletin board

15. computer

16. overhead projector

17. dry erase marker

18. chalk

19. eraser

20. pencil

21. (pencil) eraser

22. pen

23. pencil sharpener

24. marker

25. textbook

26. workbook

27. 3-ring binder / notebook

28. notebook paper

29. spiral notebook

30. dictionary

31. picture dictionary

Look at the picture.
Describe the classroom.

A: There's a chalkboard.
B: There are fifteen students.

Ask your classmates. Share the answers.

1. Do you like to raise your hand in class?
2. Do you like to listen to CDs in class?
3. Do you ever talk to the teacher?

7

Learning New Words

A. **Look up** the word.

B. **Read** the definition.

C. **Translate** the word.

D. **Check** the pronunciation.

E. **Copy** the word.

F. **Draw** a picture.

Working with Your Classmates

G. **Discuss** a problem.

H. **Brainstorm** solutions / answers.

I. **Work** in a group.

J. **Help** a classmate.

Working with a Partner

K. **Ask** a question.

L. **Answer** a question.

M. **Share** a book.

N. **Dictate** a sentence.

Following Directions

O. **Fill in** the blank.

P. **Choose** the correct answer.

Q. **Circle** the answer.

R. **Cross out** the word.

S. **Underline** the word.

T. **Match** the items.

U. **Check** the correct boxes.

V. **Label** the picture.

W. **Unscramble** the words.

X. **Put** the sentences in order.

Y. **Take out** a piece of paper.

Z. **Put away** your books.

Ask your classmates. Share the answers.

1. Do you like to work in a group?
2. Do you ever share a book?
3. Do you like to answer questions?

Think about it. Discuss.

1. How can classmates help each other?
2. Why is it important to ask questions in class?
3. How can students check their pronunciation? Explain.

Ways to Succeed

A. **Set** goals.

B. **Participate** in class.

C. **Take** notes.

D. **Study** at home.

E. **Pass** a test.

F. **Ask** for help.

G. **Make** progress.

H. **Get** good grades.

Taking a Test

1. test booklet

2. answer sheet

3. score

4. grades

I. **Clear off** your desk.

J. **Work** on your own.

K. **Bubble in** the answer.

L. **Check** your work.

M. **Erase** the mistake.

N. **Correct** the mistake.

O. **Hand in** your test.

A. **Enter** the room.

B. **Turn on** the lights.

C. **Walk** to class.

D. **Run** to class.

E. **Lift / Pick up** the books.

F. **Carry** the books.

G. **Deliver** the books.

H. **Take** a break.

I. **Eat**.

J. **Drink**.

K. **Buy** a snack.

L. **Have** a conversation.

M. **Go back** to class.

N. **Throw away** trash.

O. **Leave** the room.

P. **Turn off** the lights.

Grammar Point: present continuous

Use **be** + verb + *ing*
He **is** walk**ing**. They **are** enter**ing**.
*Note: He is run**ning**. They are leav**ing**.*

Look at the pictures.
Describe what is happening.

A: They are <u>entering the room</u>.
B: He is <u>walking</u>.

A. **start** a conversation

B. **make** small talk

C. **compliment** someone

D. **offer** something

E. **thank** someone

F. **apologize**

G. **accept** an apology

H. **invite** someone

I. **accept** an invitation

J. **decline** an invitation

K. **agree**

L. **disagree**

M. **explain** something

N. **check** your understanding

More vocabulary

request: to ask for something

accept a compliment: to thank someone for a compliment

Pair practice. Follow the directions.

1. Start a conversation with your partner.
2. Make small talk with your partner.
3. Compliment each other.

Temperature

1. Fahrenheit
2. Celsius
3. hot
4. warm
5. cool
6. cold
7. freezing
8. degrees

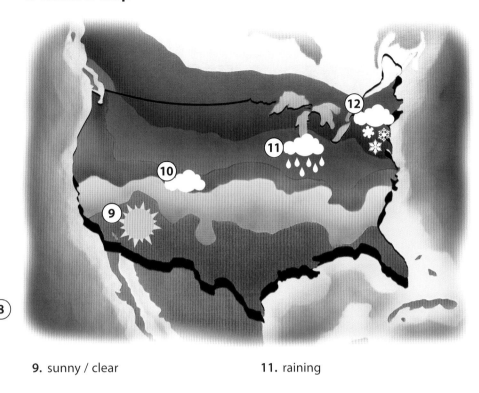

A Weather Map

9. sunny / clear
10. cloudy
11. raining
12. snowing

Weather Conditions

13. heat wave
14. smoggy
15. humid
16. thunderstorm
17. lightning
18. windy
19. dust storm
20. foggy
21. hailstorm
22. icy
23. snowstorm / blizzard

Ways to talk about the weather

It's _sunny_ in _Dallas_.
What's the temperature?
It's _108_. They're having _a heat wave_.

Pair practice. Make new conversations.

A: What's the weather like in _Chicago_?
B: It's _raining_ and it's _cold_. It's _30_ degrees.

PARTS OF A PHONE

I'll be home by 6:00.

Hello? Hello? Can you hear me?

1. receiver / handset	4. phone line	7. pound key	10. charger
2. cord	5. key pad	8. cellular phone	11. strong signal
3. phone jack	6. star key	9. antenna	12. weak signal

Hi, Bob. It's Joe. Call me.

Hi Bob. Call me.

$50 Rechargeable Phone Card
International calling made easy

1531-5471-2923-889

13. headset	15. calling card	17. answering machine	19. text message
14. wireless headset	16. access number	18. voice message	

Hi, Grandpa.

Hello, Jun.

Operator.

City and state, please.

For customer service, please press 2.

20. Internet phone call	21. operator	22. directory assistance	23. automated phone system

24. cordless phone

25. pay phone

26. TDD*

27. smart phone

Reading a Phone Bill

28. phone bill

29. area code

30. phone number

31. local call

32. long distance call

33. country code

34. city code

35. international call

Page 1 of 2

Your Phone Company Statement
October 8-November 8, 2010

Customer ID 505-555-6090

Linda Lopez
1212 Marble Lane
Roswell, NM 88203

LOCAL CALLS

DATE	NUMBER CALLED	TIME	RATE
OCT 12	505-555-2346	2:15 p.m.	day
OCT 17	505-555-7890	7:30 p.m.	night
NOV 1	505-555-6176	7:00 a.m	day
NOV 8	505-555-7890	6:30 p.m	night

Customer ID 505-555-6090
Linda Lopez

LONG DISTANCE CALLS

DATE	NUMBER CALLED	WHERE	TIME	RATE
OCT 10	212-555-1234	New York, NY	3:00 p.m.	day
OCT 31	415-555-6874	Marin, CA	9:45 p.m.	eve

INTERNATIONAL CALLS

DATE	NUMBER CALLED	WHERE		
OCT 30	56-2-555-1394	Chile		
OCT 30	81-3-555-2086	Japan		

Making a Phone Call

A. Dial the phone number.

B. Press "send".

C. Talk on the phone.

Hi!

Hi!

D. Hang up. / **Press** "end".

Making an Emergency Call

E. Dial 911.

This is Roy Chu.

F. Give your name.

There's a fire on 5th and Oak.

G. State the emergency.

Please stay on the line.

H. Stay on the line.

*telecommunication device for the deaf

Cardinal Numbers

0	zero	20	twenty
1	one	21	twenty-one
2	two	22	twenty-two
3	three	23	twenty-three
4	four	24	twenty-four
5	five	25	twenty-five
6	six	30	thirty
7	seven	40	forty
8	eight	50	fifty
9	nine	60	sixty
10	ten	70	seventy
11	eleven	80	eighty
12	twelve	90	ninety
13	thirteen	100	one hundred
14	fourteen	101	one hundred one
15	fifteen	1,000	one thousand
16	sixteen	10,000	ten thousand
17	seventeen	100,000	one hundred thousand
18	eighteen	1,000,000	one million
19	nineteen	1,000,000,000	one billion

Ordinal Numbers

1st	first	16th	sixteenth
2nd	second	17th	seventeenth
3rd	third	18th	eighteenth
4th	fourth	19th	nineteenth
5th	fifth	20th	twentieth
6th	sixth	21st	twenty-first
7th	seventh	30th	thirtieth
8th	eighth	40th	fortieth
9th	ninth	50th	fiftieth
10th	tenth	60th	sixtieth
11th	eleventh	70th	seventieth
12th	twelfth	80th	eightieth
13th	thirteenth	90th	ninetieth
14th	fourteenth	100th	one hundredth
15th	fifteenth	1,000th	one thousandth

Roman Numerals

I = 1	VII = 7	XXX = 30
II = 2	VIII = 8	XL = 40
III = 3	IX = 9	L = 50
IV = 4	X = 10	C = 100
V = 5	XV = 15	D = 500
VI = 6	XX = 20	M = 1,000

A. **divide**

B. **calculate**

C. **measure**

D. **convert**

Fractions and Decimals

1. one whole
1 = 1.00

2. one half
1/2 = .5

3. one third
1/3 = .333

4. one fourth
1/4 = .25

5. one eighth
1/8 = .125

Percents

6. calculator

7. decimal point

(8) 100 percent — 100%

(9) 75 percent — 75%

(10) 50 percent — 50%

(11) 25 percent — 25%

(12) 10 percent — 10%

0% 10% 20% 30% 40% 50% 60% 70% 80% 90% 100%

Measurement

13. ruler

14. centimeter [cm]

15. inch [in.]

Dimensions

16. height

17. length

18. depth

19. width

Equivalencies

12 inches = 1 foot

3 feet = 1 yard

1,760 yards = 1 mile

1 inch = 2.54 centimeters

1 yard = .91 meters

1 mile = 1.6 kilometers

Telling Time

1. hour

2. minutes

3. seconds

4. a.m.

5. p.m.

6. 1:00
one o'clock

7. 1:05
one-oh-five
five after one

8. 1:10
one-ten
ten after one

9. 1:15
one-fifteen
a quarter after one

10. 1:20
one-twenty
twenty after one

11. 1:30
one-thirty
half past one

12. 1:40
one-forty
twenty to two

13. 1:45
one-forty-five
a quarter to two

Times of Day

14. sunrise

15. morning

16. noon

17. afternoon

18. sunset

19. evening

20. night

21. midnight

Ways to talk about time

I wake up at 6:30 a.m.
I wake up at 6:30 in the morning.
I wake up at 6:30.

Pair practice. Make new conversations.

A: *What time do you wake up on weekdays?*
B: *At 6:30 a.m. How about you?*
A: *I wake up at 7:00.*

22. early

23. on time

24. late

25. daylight saving time

26. standard time

Time Zones

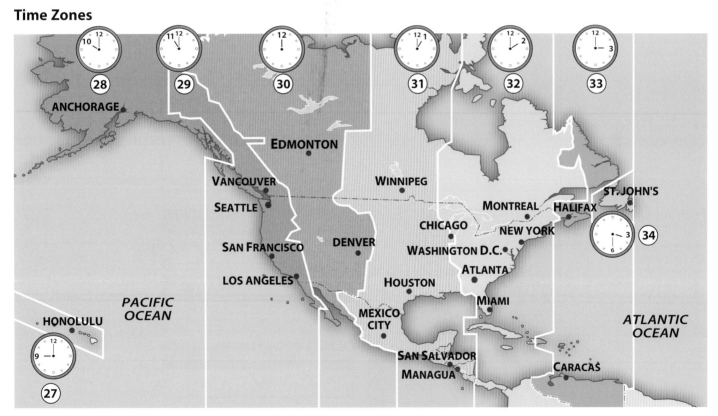

27. Hawaii-Aleutian time

28. Alaska time

29. Pacific time

30. Mountain time

31. Central time

32. Eastern time

33. Atlantic time

34. Newfoundland time

Ask your classmates. Share the answers.

1. When do you watch television? study? relax?
2. Do you like to stay up after midnight?
3. Do you like to wake up late on weekends?

Think about it. Discuss.

1. What is your favorite time of day? Why?
2. Do you think daylight saving time is a good idea? Why or why not?

19

1. date
2. day
3. month
4. year

5. today
6. tomorrow
7. yesterday

Days of the Week

8. Sunday
9. Monday
10. Tuesday
11. Wednesday
12. Thursday
13. Friday
14. Saturday

15. week
16. weekdays
17. weekend

MAY

SUN	MON	TUE	WED	THU	FRI	SAT
1	2	3	4	5	6	7
8	9	10	11	12	13	14
15	16	17	18	19	20	21
22	23	24	25	26	27	28
29	30	31				

Frequency

18. last week
19. this week
20. next week

MAY

SUN	MON	TUE	WED	THU	FRI	SAT
X1	X2	X3	X4	X5	X6	X7
8	9	10	11	12	13	14
15	16	17	18	19	20	21
22	23	24	25	26	27	28

SUN	MON	TUE	WED	THU	FRI	SAT
✓	✓	✓	✓	✓	✓	✓

21. every day / daily

SUN	MON	TUE	WED	THU	FRI	SAT
	✓					

22. once a week

SUN	MON	TUE	WED	THU	FRI	SAT
		✓		✓		

23. twice a week

SUN	MON	TUE	WED	THU	FRI	SAT
	✓	✓		✓		

24. three times a week

Ways to say the date

Today is _May 10th_. It's the _tenth_.
Yesterday was _May 9th_.
The party is on _May 21st_.

Pair practice. Make new conversations.

A: The _test_ is on _Friday_, _June 14th_.
B: Did you say _Friday_, the _fourteenth_?
A: Yes, the _fourteenth_.

Months of the Year

(25) JAN

SUN	MON	TUE	WED	THU	FRI	SAT
					1	2
3	4	5	6	7	8	9
10	11	12	13	14	15	16
17	18	19	20	21	22	23
24/31	25	26	27	28	29	30

(26) FEB

SUN	MON	TUE	WED	THU	FRI	SAT
	1	2	3	4	5	6
7	8	9	10	11	12	13
14	15	16	17	18	19	20
21	22	23	24	25	26	27
28						

(27) MAR

SUN	MON	TUE	WED	THU	FRI	SAT
	1	2	3	4	5	6
7	8	9	10	11	12	13
14	15	16	17	18	19	20
21	22	23	24	25	26	27
28	29	30	31			

(28) APR

SUN	MON	TUE	WED	THU	FRI	SAT
				1	2	3
4	5	6	7	8	9	10
11	12	13	14	15	16	17
18	19	20	21	22	23	24
25	26	27	28	29	30	

(29) MAY

SUN	MON	TUE	WED	THU	FRI	SAT
						1
2	3	4	5	6	7	8
9	10	11	12	13	14	15
16	17	18	19	20	21	22
23/30	24/31	25	26	27	28	29

(30) JUN

SUN	MON	TUE	WED	THU	FRI	SAT
		1	2	3	4	5
6	7	8	9	10	11	12
13	14	15	16	17	18	19
20	21	22	23	24	25	26
27	28	29	30			

(31) JUL

SUN	MON	TUE	WED	THU	FRI	SAT
				1	2	3
4	5	6	7	8	9	10
11	12	13	14	15	16	17
18	19	20	21	22	23	24
25	26	27	28	29	30	31

(32) AUG

SUN	MON	TUE	WED	THU	FRI	SAT
1	2	3	4	5	6	7
8	9	10	11	12	13	14
15	16	17	18	19	20	21
22	23	24	25	26	27	28
29	30	31				

(33) SEP

SUN	MON	TUE	WED	THU	FRI	SAT
			1	2	3	4
5	6	7	8	9	10	11
12	13	14	15	16	17	18
19	20	21	22	23	24	25
26	27	28	29	30		

(34) OCT

SUN	MON	TUE	WED	THU	FRI	SAT
					1	2
3	4	5	6	7	8	9
10	11	12	13	14	15	16
17	18	19	20	21	22	23
24/31	25	26	27	28	29	30

(35) NOV

SUN	MON	TUE	WED	THU	FRI	SAT
	1	2	3	4	5	6
7	8	9	10	11	12	13
14	15	16	17	18	19	20
21	22	23	24	25	26	27
28	29	30				

(36) DEC

SUN	MON	TUE	WED	THU	FRI	SAT
			1	2	3	4
5	6	7	8	9	10	11
12	13	14	15	16	17	18
19	20	21	22	23	24	25
26	27	28	29	30	31	

Months of the Year

25. January

26. February

27. March

28. April

29. May

30. June

31. July

32. August

33. September

34. October

35. November

36. December

Seasons

37. spring

38. summer

39. fall / autumn

40. winter

Dictate to your partner. Take turns.

A: *Write Monday.*

B: *Is it spelled M-o-n-d-a-y?*

A: *Yes, that's right.*

Ask your classmates. Share the answers.

1. What is your favorite day of the week? Why?
2. What is your busiest day of the week? Why?
3. What is your favorite season of the year? Why?

1. birthday

2. wedding

3. anniversary

4. appointment

5. parent-teacher conference

6. vacation

7. religious holiday

8. legal holiday

Legal Holidays

Happy New Year! JAN 1

I have a dream. JAN

FEB

MAY

JUL 4

SEP

OCT

PROUD TO WORK

DEC 25

NOV

NOV

9. New Year's Day

10. Martin Luther King Jr. Day

11. Presidents' Day

12. Memorial Day

13. Fourth of July / Independence Day

14. Labor Day

15. Columbus Day

16. Veterans Day

17. Thanksgiving

18. Christmas

Pair practice. Make new conversations.

A: *When is your <u>birthday</u>?*
B: *It's on <u>January 31st</u>. How about you?*
A: *It's on <u>December 22nd</u>.*

Ask your classmates. Share the answers.

1. What are the legal holidays in your native country?
2. When is Labor Day in your native country?
3. When do you celebrate the New Year in your native country?

1. **little** hand

2. **big** hand

3. **fast** driver

4. **slow** driver

5. **hard** chair

6. **soft** chair

7. **thick** book

8. **thin** book

9. **full** glass

10. **empty** glass

11. **noisy** children / **loud** children

12. **quiet** children

13. **heavy** box

14. **light** box

15. **same** color

16. **different** colors

17. **good** dog

18. **bad** dog

19. **expensive** ring

20. **cheap** ring

21. **beautiful** view

22. **ugly** view

23. **easy** problem

24. **difficult** problem / **hard** problem

$1 + 1 = 2$

$$x^2 - 22\tfrac{1}{2}x = 8\tfrac{1}{3}x^2 - 11\tfrac{2}{3}$$

Ask your classmates. Share the answers.

1. Are you a slow driver or a fast driver?
2. Do you prefer a hard bed or a soft bed?
3. Do you like loud parties or quiet parties?

Use the new words.

Look at page 150–151. Describe the things you see.

A: *The street* is *hard*.
B: *The truck* is *heavy*.

Basic Colors

1. red

2. yellow

3. blue

4. orange

5. green

6. purple

7. pink

8. violet

9. turquoise

10. dark blue

11. light blue

12. bright blue

Neutral Colors

13. black

14. white

15. gray

16. cream / ivory

17. brown

18. beige / tan

Ask your classmates. Share the answers.

1. What colors are you wearing today?
2. What colors do you like?
3. Is there a color you don't like? What is it?

Use the new words. Look at pages 86–87.
Take turns naming the colors you see.

A: *His shirt is blue.*
B: *Her shoes are white.*

1. The yellow sweaters are **on the left**.

2. The purple sweaters are **in the middle**.

3. The brown sweaters are **on the right**.

4. The red sweaters are **above** the blue sweaters.

5. The blue sweaters are **below** the red sweaters.

6. The turquoise sweater is **in** the box.

7. The white sweater is **in front of** the black sweater.

8. The black sweater is **behind** the white sweater.

9. The violet sweater is **next to** the gray sweater.

10. The gray sweater is **under** the orange sweater.

11. The orange sweater is **on** the gray sweater.

12. The green sweater is **between** the pink sweaters.

More vocabulary

near: in the same area
far from: not near

Role play. Make new conversations.

A: *Excuse me. Where are the <u>red</u> sweaters?*
B: *They're <u>on the left</u>, <u>above</u> the <u>blue</u> sweaters.*
A: *Thanks very much.*

25

Coins

1. $.01 = 1¢
a penny / 1 cent

2. $.05 = 5¢
a nickel / 5 cents

3. $.10 = 10¢
a dime / 10 cents

4. $.25 = 25¢
a quarter / 25 cents

5. $.50 = 50¢
a half dollar

6. $1.00
a dollar coin

Bills

7. $1.00
a dollar

8. $5.00
five dollars

9. $10.00
ten dollars

10. $20.00
twenty dollars

11. $50.00
fifty dollars

12. $100.00
one hundred dollars

A. **Get** change.

B. **Borrow** money.   C. **Lend** money.

D. **Pay back** the money.

Pair practice. Make new conversations.

A: *Do you have change for a dollar?*
B: *Sure. How about two quarters and five dimes?*
A: *Perfect!*

Think about it. Discuss.

1. Is it a good idea to lend money to a friend? Why or why not?
2. Is it better to carry a dollar or four quarters? Why?
3. Do you prefer dollar coins or dollar bills? Why?

Ways to Pay

A. **pay** cash

B. **use** a credit card

C. **use** a debit card

D. **write** a (personal) check

E. **use** a gift card

F. **cash** a traveler's check

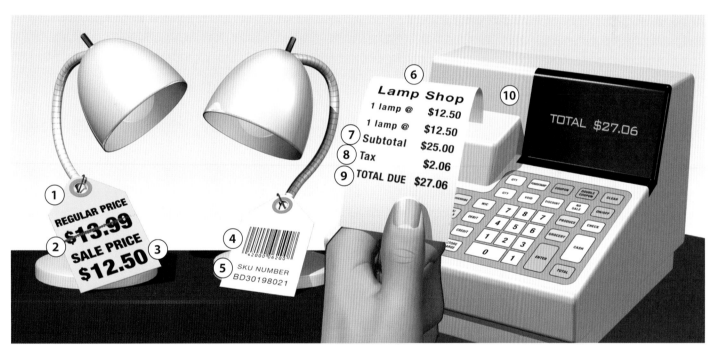

1. price tag
2. regular price
3. sale price
4. bar code
5. SKU number
6. receipt
7. price / cost
8. sales tax
9. total
10. cash register

G. **buy / pay for**

H. **return**

I. **exchange**

1. twins
2. sweater
3. matching
4. disappointed
5. navy blue
6. happy
A. **shop**
B. **keep**

Look at the pictures.
What do you see?

Answer the questions.

1. Who is the woman shopping for?

2. Does she buy matching sweaters or different sweaters?

3. How does Anya feel about her green sweater? What does she do?

4. What does Manda do with her sweater?

📖 Read the story.

Same and Different

Mrs. Kumar likes to <u>shop</u> for her <u>twins</u>. Today she's looking at <u>sweaters</u>. There are many different colors on sale. Mrs. Kumar chooses two <u>matching</u> green sweaters.

The next day, Manda and Anya open their gifts. Manda likes the green sweater, but Anya is <u>disappointed</u>. Mrs. Kumar understands the problem. Anya wants to be different.

Manda <u>keeps</u> her sweater. But Anya goes to the store. She exchanges her green sweater for a <u>navy blue</u> sweater. It's an easy answer to Anya's problem. Now the twins can be warm, <u>happy</u>, and different.

Think about it.

1. Do you like to shop for other people? Why or why not?

2. Imagine you are Anya. Would you keep the sweater or exchange it? Why?

1. man

2. woman

3. women

4. men

5. senior citizen

Listen and point. Take turns.

A: *Point to a <u>woman</u>.*
B: *Point to a <u>senior citizen</u>.*
A: *Point to an <u>infant</u>.*

Dictate to your partner. Take turns.

A: *Write <u>woman</u>.*
B: *Is that spelled <u>w-o-m-a-n</u>?*
A: *Yes, that's right, <u>woman</u>.*

6. infant

7. baby

8. toddler

9. 6-year-old boy

10. 10-year-old girl

11. teenager / teen

Ways to talk about age

1 month – 3 months old = **infant**

18 months – 3 years old = **toddler**

3 years old – 12 years old = **child**

13 – 19 years old = **teenager**

18+ years old = **adult**

62+ years old = **senior citizen**

Pair practice. Make new conversations.

A: *How old is Sandra?*

B: *She's thirteen years old.*

A: *Wow, she's a teenager now!*

Age

1. young
2. middle-aged
3. elderly

Height

4. tall
5. average height
6. short

Weight

7. heavy / fat
8. average weight
9. thin / slender

Disabilities

10. physically challenged
11. sight impaired / blind
12. hearing impaired / deaf

Prepositions of Motion p.153

Appearance

13. attractive   14. cute   15. pregnant   16. mole   17. pierced ear

18. tattoo

Ways to describe people

He's a <u>heavy</u>, <u>young</u> man.
She's a <u>pregnant</u> woman with <u>a mole</u>.
He's <u>sight impaired</u>.

Use the new words. Look at pages 2–3.
Describe the people and point. Take turns.

A: *He's a <u>tall</u>, <u>thin</u>, <u>middle-aged</u> man.*
B: *She's a <u>short</u>, <u>average-weight</u> <u>young</u> woman.*

1. short hair
2. shoulder-length hair
3. long hair
4. part
5. mustache

6. beard
7. sideburns
8. bangs
9. straight hair
10. wavy hair

11. curly hair
12. bald
13. gray hair
14. corn rows
15. red hair

16. black hair
17. blond hair
18. brown hair
19. rollers
20. scissors

21. comb
22. brush
23. blow dryer

Style Hair

A. **cut** hair

B. **perm** hair

C. **set** hair

D. **color** hair / **dye** hair

Ways to talk about hair

Describe hair in this order: length, style, and then color.
She has <u>long</u>, <u>straight</u>, <u>brown</u> hair.

Role play. Talk to a stylist.

A: *I need a new hairstyle.*
B: *How about <u>short</u> and <u>straight</u>?*
A: *Great. Do you think I should <u>dye</u> it?*

33

1. grandmother
2. grandfather
3. mother
4. father
5. sister
6. brother
7. aunt
8. uncle
9. cousin

Tim Lee's Family

GRANDPARENTS

PARENTS

CHILDREN

Immediate Family

10. mother-in-law
11. father-in-law
12. wife
13. husband
14. daughter
15. son
16. sister-in-law
17. brother-in-law
18. niece
19. nephew

Ana Garcia's Family

Extended Family

More vocabulary

Tim is Min and Lu's **grandson**.
Lily and Emily are Min and Lu's **granddaughters**.
Alex is Min's youngest **grandchild**.

Ana is Tito's **wife**.
Ana is Eva and Sam's **daughter-in-law**.
Carlos is Eva and Sam's **son-in-law**.

34

20. married couple

21. divorced couple

22. single mother

23. single father

Carol, Bruce, and Lisa

Lisa, Age 4

Lisa Green's Family

24. remarried

25. stepfather

26. stepmother

27. half sister

28. half brother

29. stepsister

30. stepbrother

Lisa, Age 7

Rick   Carol   Bruce   Sue

Lisa, Today

Mary   David   Kim   Bill

More vocabulary

Bruce is Carol's **former husband** or **ex-husband**.
Carol is Bruce's **former wife** or **ex-wife**.
Lisa is the **stepdaughter** of both Rick and Sue.

Look at the pictures.
Name the people.

A: *Who is* <u>*Lisa's*</u> <u>*half sister*</u>?
B: <u>*Mary*</u> *is. Who is* <u>*Lisa's*</u> <u>*stepsister*</u>?

A. hold

B. nurse

C. feed

D. rock

E. undress

F. bathe

G. change a diaper

H. dress

I. comfort

J. praise

K. discipline

L. buckle up

M. play with

N. read to

O. sing a lullaby

P. kiss goodnight

Look at the pictures.
Describe what is happening.

A: *She's changing her baby's diaper*.
B: *He's kissing his son goodnight*.

Ask your classmates. Share the answers.
1. Do you like to take care of children?
2. Do you prefer to read to children or play with them?
3. Can you sing a lullaby? Which one?

1. bottle
2. nipple
3. formula
4. baby food

5. bib
6. high chair
7. diaper pail
8. cloth diaper

9. safety pins
10. disposable diaper
11. training pants
12. potty seat

13. baby lotion
14. baby powder
15. wipes

16. baby bag
17. baby carrier
18. stroller

19. car safety seat
20. carriage
21. rocking chair

22. nursery rhymes
23. teddy bear
24. pacifier

25. teething ring
26. rattle
27. night light

Dictate to your partner. Take turns.

A: *Write pacifier.*
B: *Was that pacifier, p-a-c-i-f-i-e-r?*
A: *Yes, that's right.*

Think about it. Discuss.

1. How can parents discipline toddlers? teens?
2. What are some things you can say to praise a child?
3. Why are nursery rhymes important for young children?

37

A. **wake up**

B. **get up**

C. **take** a shower

D. **get dressed**

E. **eat** breakfast

F. **make** lunch

G. **take** the children to school /
   drop off the kids

H. **take** the bus to school

I. **drive** to work / **go** to work

J. **go** to class

K. **work**

L. **go** to the grocery store

M. **pick up** the kids

N. **leave** work

Grammar Point: third person singular

For *he* and *she*, add **-s** or **-es** to the verb:

He wake**s** up.	He watch**es** TV.
He get**s** up.	She go**es** to the store.

These verbs are different (irregular):

*Be: She **is** in school at 10:00 a.m.*

*Have: He **has** dinner at 6:30 p.m.*

O. **clean** the house

P. **exercise**

Q. **cook** dinner / **make** dinner

R. **come** home / **get** home

S. **have** dinner / **eat** dinner

T. **do** homework

U. **relax**

V. **read** the paper

W. **check** email

X. **watch** TV

Y. **go** to bed

Z. **go** to sleep

Pair practice. Make new conversations.

A: *When does he go to work?*
B: *He goes to work at 8:00 a.m. When does she go to class?*
A: *She goes to class at 10:00 a.m.*

Ask your classmates. Share the answers.

1. Who cooks dinner in your family?
2. Who goes to the grocery store?
3. Who goes to work?

A. **be born** — 1935

B. **start** school — 1940

1. birth certificate

2. Resident Alien card / green card

C. **immigrate** — 1950

D. **graduate** — 1953

3. diploma

E. **learn** to drive — 1953

F. **get** a job — 1954

4. driver's license

5. Social Security card

G. **become** a citizen — 1954

H. **fall in love** — 1955

6. Certificate of Naturalization

Grammar Point: past tense

start
learn } +ed
travel

immigrate   retire
graduate   die } +d

These verbs are different (irregular):

be – was   go – went   buy – bought
get – got   have – had
become – became   fall – fell

I. **go** to college — 1956

J. **get** engaged — 1958

7. college degree

K. **get** married — 1959

L. **have** a baby — 1961

8. marriage license

M. **buy** a home — 1965

N. **become** a grandparent — 1986

9. deed

O. **retire** — 2000

P. **travel** — 2005

10. passport

Q. **volunteer** — 2006

R. **die** — 2008

11. death certificate

More vocabulary

When a husband dies, his wife becomes a **widow**.
When a wife dies, her husband becomes a **widower**.

Ask your classmates. Share the answers.

1. When did you start school?
2. When did you get your first job?
3. Do you want to travel?

41

1. hot
2. thirsty
3. sleepy
4. cold
5. hungry
6. full / satisfied

7. disgusted
8. calm
9. uncomfortable
10. nervous

11. in pain
12. sick
13. worried
14. well
15. relieved

16. hurt
17. lonely
18. in love

Pair practice. Make new conversations.

A: *How are you doing?*
B: *I'm hungry. How about you?*
A: *I'm hungry and thirsty, too!*

Use the new words.
Look at pages 40–41. Describe what each person is feeling.

A: *Martin is excited.*
B: *Martin's mother is proud.*

19. sad

20. homesick

21. proud

22. excited

23. scared / afraid

24. embarrassed

25. bored

26. confused

27. frustrated

28. upset

29. angry

30. surprised

31. happy

32. tired

Ask your classmates. Share the answers.

1. Do you ever feel homesick?
2. What makes you feel frustrated?
3. Describe a time when you were very happy.

More vocabulary

exhausted: very tired

furious: very angry

humiliated: very embarrassed

overjoyed: very happy

starving: very hungry

terrified: very scared

1. banner
2. baseball game
3. opinion
4. balloons
5. glad
6. relatives

A. **laugh**
B. **misbehave**

I think large families are best.

Look at the picture.
What do you see?

Answer the questions.

1. How many relatives are there at this reunion?

2. How many children are there? Which children are misbehaving?

3. What are people doing at this reunion?

📖 **Read the story.**

A Family Reunion

Ben Lu has a lot of <u>relatives</u> and they're all at his house. Today is the Lu family reunion.

There is a lot of good food. There are also <u>balloons</u> and a <u>banner</u>. And this year there are four new babies!

People are having a good time at the reunion. Ben's grandfather and his aunt are talking about the <u>baseball game</u>. His cousins <u>are laughing</u>. His mother-in-law is giving her <u>opinion</u>. And many of the children <u>are misbehaving</u>.

Ben looks at his family and smiles. He loves his relatives, but he's <u>glad</u> the reunion is once a year.

Think about it.

1. Do you like to have large parties? Why or why not?

2. Imagine you see a little girl at a party. She's misbehaving. What do you do? What do you say?

The Home

1. roof

2. bedroom

3. door

4. bathroom

5. kitchen

6. floor

7. dining area

Listen and point. Take turns.

A: *Point to the kitchen.*
B: *Point to the living room.*
A: *Point to the basement.*

Dictate to your partner. Take turns.

A: *Write kitchen.*
B: *Was that k-i-t-c-h-e-n?*
A: *Yes, that's right, kitchen.*

8. attic

9. kids' bedroom

10. baby's room

11. window

12. living room

13. basement

14. garage

Ways to give locations

I'm home.
I'm in the kitchen.
I'm on the roof.

Pair practice. Make new conversations.

A: *Where's the man?*
B: *He's in the attic. Where's the teenager?*
A: *She's in the laundry room.*

47

1. Internet listing

West Rentals
1 Bedroom
$900 / Month
Call for info:
818-555-4949

2. classified ad

Apartment For Rent
2 bdrm 2ba city apt
Unfurn Sunny kit
Util incl
$850/mo
Call mgr eves
212-555-2368
Near centenial Plaza

Abbreviations

apt = apartment

bdrm = bedroom

ba = bathroom

kit = kitchen

yd = yard

util = utilities

incl = included

mo = month

furn = furnished

unfurn = unfurnished

mgr = manager

eves = evenings

3. furnished apartment

4. unfurnished apartment

Gas **Water** **Electricity** **Phone** **Cable** **DSL**

5. utilities

Renting an Apartment

A. **Call** the manager.

Are utilities included?

No, they aren't.

B. **Ask** about the features.

C. **Submit** an application.

D. **Sign** the rental agreement.

E. **Pay** the first and last month's rent.

F. **Move in**.

More vocabulary

lease: a monthly or yearly rental agreement
redecorate: to change the paint and furniture in a home
move out: to pack and leave a home

Ask your classmates. Share the answers.

1. How did you find your home?
2. Do you like to paint or arrange furniture?
3. Does gas or electricity cost more for you?

Buying a House

G. Meet with a realtor.

H. Look at houses.

I. Make an offer.

J. Get a loan.

K. Take ownership.

L. Make a mortgage payment.

Moving In

M. Pack.

N. Unpack.

O. Put the utilities in your name.

P. Paint.

Q. Arrange the furniture.

R. Meet the neighbors.

Ways to ask about a home's features

Are utilities included?
Is the kitchen large and sunny?
Are the neighbors quiet?

Role play. Talk to an apartment manager.

A: Hi. I'm calling about the apartment.
B: OK. It's unfurnished and rent is $800 a month.
A: Are utilities included?

49

1. apartment building
2. fire escape
3. playground
4. roof garden

Entrance

Apartment Available
2BD + 2BA
555-4263

5. intercom / speaker
6. tenant
7. vacancy sign
8. manager / superintendent

Lobby

9. elevator
10. stairs / stairway
11. mailboxes

Basement

LAUNDRY ROOM

SOAP SOFTENER

RECREATION ROOM

GARAGE

12. washer
13. dryer
14. big-screen TV
15. pool table
16. security gate
17. storage locker
18. parking space
19. security camera

Grammar Point: *there is / there are*

singular: there is   **plural:** there are
There is *a recreation room in the basement.*
There are *mailboxes in the lobby.*

Look at the pictures.
Describe the apartment building.

A: *There's <u>a pool table</u> in the recreation room.*
B: *There are <u>parking spaces</u> in the garage.*

APARTMENT COMPLEX

20. balcony	22. swimming pool	24. alley
21. courtyard	23. trash bin	

Hallway

FIRE EXIT

25. emergency exit   26. trash chute

Rental Office

27. landlord   28. lease / rental agreement

An Apartment Entryway

It's Joe.

Come up.

29. smoke detector	31. buzzer	33. door chain
30. key	32. peephole	34. dead-bolt lock

More vocabulary

upstairs: the floor(s) above you
downstairs: the floor(s) below you
fire exit: another name for emergency exit

Role play. Talk to a landlord.

A: *Is there a swimming pool in this complex?*
B: *Yes, there is. It's near the courtyard.*
A: *Is there…?*

1. the city / an urban area   2. the suburbs   3. a small town / a village   4. the country / a rural area

5. condominium / condo

6. townhouse

7. mobile home

8. college dormitory / dorm

9. farm

10. ranch

11. senior housing

12. nursing home

13. shelter

More vocabulary

co-op: an apartment building owned by residents
duplex: a house divided into two homes
two-story house: a house with two floors

Think about it. Discuss.

1. What's good and bad about these places to live?
2. How are small towns different from cities?
3. How do shelters help people in need?

Front Yard and House

Front Porch

1. mailbox	4. gutter	7. garage door
2. front walk	5. chimney	8. driveway
3. steps	6. satellite dish	9. gate

10. storm door	13. porch light
11. front door	14. doorbell
12. doorknob	15. screen door

Backyard

16. patio	19. patio furniture	22. sprinkler	25. compost pile	A. **take** a nap
17. grill	20. flower bed	23. hammock	26. lawn	B. **garden**
18. sliding glass door	21. hose	24. garbage can	27. vegetable garden	

1. cabinet	8. dishwasher	15. toaster oven	22. counter
2. shelf	9. refrigerator	16. pot	23. drawer
3. paper towels	10. freezer	17. teakettle	24. pan
4. sink	11. coffeemaker	18. stove	25. electric mixer
5. dish rack	12. blender	19. burner	26. food processor
6. toaster	13. microwave	20. oven	27. cutting board
7. garbage disposal	14. electric can opener	21. broiler	28. mixing bowl

Ways to talk about location using *on* and *in*

Use **on** for the counter, shelf, burner, stove, and cutting board. *It's **on** the counter.* Use **in** for the dishwasher, oven, sink, and drawer. *Put it **in** the sink.*

Pair practice. Make new conversations.

A: *Please move <u>the blender</u>.*
B: *Sure. Do you want it <u>in the cabinet</u>?*
A: *No, put it <u>on the counter</u>.*

1. dish / plate	**7.** coffee mug	**13.** salt and pepper shakers	**19.** fan
2. bowl	**8.** dining room chair	**14.** sugar bowl	**20.** platter
3. fork	**9.** dining room table	**15.** creamer	**21.** serving bowl
4. knife	**10.** napkin	**16.** teapot	**22.** hutch
5. spoon	**11.** placemat	**17.** tray	**23.** vase
6. teacup	**12.** tablecloth	**18.** light fixture	**24.** buffet

Ways to make requests at the table

May I have the sugar bowl?
Would you pass the creamer, please?
Could I have a coffee mug?

Role play. Request items at the table.

A: *What do you need?*
B: *Could I have a coffee mug?*
A: *Certainly. And would you...*

55

1. love seat	7. DVD player	13. fireplace	19. coffee table
2. throw pillow	8. stereo system	14. end table	20. candle
3. basket	9. painting	15. floor lamp	21. candle holder
4. houseplant	10. wall	16. drapes	22. armchair / easy chair
5. entertainment center	11. mantle	17. window	23. magazine holder
6. TV (television)	12. fire screen	18. sofa / couch	24. carpet

Use the new words.
Look at pages 44–45. Name the things in the room.

A: There's _a TV_.
B: There's _a carpet_.

More vocabulary
light bulb: the light inside a lamp
lampshade: the part of the lamp that covers the light bulb
sofa cushions: the pillows that are part of the sofa

1. hamper	**8.** faucet	**15.** towel rack	**22.** medicine cabinet
2. bathtub	**9.** hot water	**16.** bath towel	**23.** toothbrush
3. soap dish	**10.** cold water	**17.** hand towel	**24.** toothbrush holder
4. soap	**11.** grab bar	**18.** mirror	**25.** sink
5. rubber mat	**12.** tile	**19.** toilet paper	**26.** wastebasket
6. washcloth	**13.** showerhead	**20.** toilet brush	**27.** scale
7. drain	**14.** shower curtain	**21.** toilet	**28.** bath mat

More vocabulary

stall shower: a shower without a bathtub
half bath: a bathroom with no shower or tub
linen closet: a closet for towels and sheets

Ask your classmates. Share the answers.

1. Is your toothbrush on the sink or in the medicine cabinet?
2. Do you have a bathtub or a shower?
3. Do you have a shower curtain or a shower door?

57

1. dresser / bureau	8. mini-blinds	15. blanket	22. rug
2. drawer	9. bed	16. quilt	23. night table / nightstand
3. photos	10. headboard	17. dust ruffle	24. alarm clock
4. picture frame	11. pillow	18. bed frame	25. lamp
5. closet	12. fitted sheet	19. box spring	26. lampshade
6. full-length mirror	13. flat sheet	20. mattress	27. light switch
7. curtains	14. pillowcase	21. wood floor	28. outlet

Look at the pictures.
Describe the bedroom.

A: *There's a lamp on the nightstand.*
B: *There's a mirror in the closet.*

Ask your classmates. Share the answers.
1. Do you prefer a hard or a soft mattress?
2. Do you prefer mini-blinds or curtains?
3. How many pillows do you like on your bed?

Furniture and Accessories

1. changing table
2. changing pad
3. crib
4. bumper pad
5. mobile
6. chest of drawers
7. baby monitor
8. wallpaper
9. bunk beds
10. safety rail
11. bedspread

Toys and Games

12. ball
13. coloring book
14. crayons
15. stuffed animals
16. toy chest
17. puzzle
18. dollhouse
19. blocks
20. cradle
21. doll

Pair practice. Make conversations.

A: *Where's the changing pad?*
B: *It's on the changing table.*

Think about it. Discuss.

1. Which toys help children learn? How?
2. Which toys are good for older and younger children?
3. What safety features does this room need? Why?

A. **dust** the furniture

B. **recycle** the newspapers

C. **clean** the oven

D. **mop** the floor

E. **polish** the furniture

F. **make** the bed

G. **put away** the toys

H. **vacuum** the carpet

I. **wash** the windows

J. **sweep** the floor

K. **scrub** the sink

L. **empty** the trash

M. **wash** the dishes

N. **dry** the dishes

O. **wipe** the counter

P. **change** the sheets

Q. **take out** the garbage

Pair practice. Make new conversations.

A: *Let's clean this place. First, I'll* <u>sweep the floor</u>.

B: *I'll* <u>mop the floor</u> *when you finish.*

Ask your classmates. Share the answers.

1. Who does the housework in your home?
2. How often do you wash the windows?
3. When should kids start to do housework?

1. feather duster
2. recycling bin
3. oven cleaner
4. rubber gloves
5. steel-wool soap pads
6. sponge mop
7. bucket / pail
8. furniture polish

9. rags
10. vacuum cleaner
11. vacuum cleaner attachments
12. vacuum cleaner bag
13. stepladder
14. glass cleaner
15. squeegee
16. broom

17. dustpan
18. cleanser
19. sponge
20. scrub brush
21. dishwashing liquid
22. dish towel
23. disinfectant wipes
24. trash bags

Ways to ask for something

Please hand me the squeegee.
Can you get me the broom?
I need the sponge mop.

Pair practice. Make new conversations.

A: *Please hand me the sponge mop.*
B: *Here you go. Do you need the bucket?*
A: *Yes, please. Can you get me the rubber gloves, too?*

1. The water heater is **not working**.

2. The power is **out**.

3. The roof is **leaking**.

4. The tile is **cracked**.

5. The window is **broken**.

6. The lock is **broken**.

7. The steps are **broken**.

8. roofer

9. electrician

10. repair person

11. locksmith

12. carpenter

13. fuse box

14. gas meter

More vocabulary

fix: to repair something that is broken
pests: termites, fleas, rats, etc.
exterminate: to kill household pests

Pair practice. Make new conversations.

A: *The faucet is <u>leaking</u>.*
B: *Let's call <u>the plumber</u>. He can fix it.*

15. The furnace is **broken**.

16. The pipes are **frozen**.

17. The faucet is **dripping**.

18. The sink is **overflowing**.

19. The toilet is **stopped up**.

20. plumber

21. exterminator

22. termites

23. ants

24. bedbugs

25. fleas

26. cockroaches / roaches

27. rats

28. mice*

***Note:** one mouse, two mice

Ways to ask about repairs

How much will this repair cost?
When can you begin?
How long will the repair take?

Role play. Talk to a repair person.

A: *Can you fix <u>the roof</u>?*
B: *Yes, but it will take <u>two weeks</u>.*
A: *How much will the repair cost?*

1. roommates

2. party

3. music

4. DJ

5. noise

6. irritated

7. rules

8. mess

9. invitation

A. **dance**

Look at the pictures. What do you see?

Answer the questions.

1. What happened in apartment 2B? How many people were there?

2. How did the neighbor feel? Why?

3. What rules did they write at the tenant meeting?

4. What did the roommates do after the tenant meeting?

 Read the story.

The Tenant Meeting

Sally Lopez and Tina Green are roommates. They live in apartment 2B. One night they had a big party with music and a DJ. There was a mess in the hallway. Their neighbors were very unhappy. Mr. Clark in 2A was very irritated. He hates noise!

The next day there was a tenant meeting. Everyone wanted rules about parties and loud music. The girls were very embarrassed.

After the meeting, the girls cleaned the mess in the hallway. Then they gave each neighbor an invitation to a new party. Everyone had a good time at the rec room party. Now the tenants have two new rules and a new place to dance.

Think about it.

1. What are the most important rules in an apartment building? Why?

2. Imagine you are the neighbor in 2A. What do you say to Tina and Sally?

65

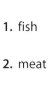

1. fish

2. meat

3. chicken

4. cheese

5. milk

6. butter

7. eggs

8. vegetables

Listen and point. Take turns.

A: *Point to the vegetables.*

B: *Point to the bread.*

A: *Point to the fruit.*

Pair Dictation

A: *Write vegetables.*

B: *Please spell vegetables for me.*

A: *V-e-g-e-t-a-b-l-e-s.*

9. fruit

10. rice

11. bread

12. pasta

13. grocery bag

14. shopping list

15. coupons

✓ milk
✓ bread
✓ lettuce
✓ grapes

Ways to talk about food.

Do we need <u>eggs</u>?

Do we have any <u>pasta</u>?

We have some <u>vegetables</u>, but we need <u>fruit</u>.

Role play. Talk about your shopping list.

A: *Do we need eggs?*

B: *No, we have some.*

A: *Do we have any...*

SPECIAL
2 BUNCHES for $1.00

1. apples
2. bananas
3. grapes
4. pears
5. oranges
6. grapefruit
7. lemons
8. limes

9. tangerines
10. peaches
11. cherries
12. apricots
13. plums
14. strawberries
15. raspberries
16. blueberries

17. blackberries
18. watermelons
19. melons
20. papayas
21. mangoes
22. kiwi
23. pineapples
24. coconuts

25. raisins
26. prunes
27. figs
28. dates
29. a bunch of bananas
30. **ripe** banana
31. **unripe** banana
32. **rotten** banana

Pair practice. Make new conversations.

A: *What's your favorite fruit?*
B: *I like <u>apples</u>. Do you?*
A: *I prefer <u>bananas</u>.*

Ask your classmates. Share the answers.

1. Which fruit do you put in a fruit salad?
2. What kinds of fruit are common in your native country?
3. What kinds of fruit are in your kitchen right now?

1. lettuce
2. cabbage
3. carrots
4. radishes
5. beets
6. tomatoes
7. bell peppers
8. string beans

9. celery
10. cucumbers
11. spinach
12. corn
13. broccoli
14. cauliflower
15. bok choy
16. turnips

17. potatoes
18. sweet potatoes
19. onions
20. green onions / scallions
21. peas
22. artichokes
23. eggplants
24. squash

25. zucchini
26. asparagus
27. mushrooms
28. parsley
29. chili peppers
30. garlic
31. a **bag of** lettuce
32. a **head of** lettuce

Pair practice. Make new conversations.

A: *Do you eat <u>broccoli</u>?*
B: *Yes. I like most vegetables, but not <u>peppers</u>.*
A: *Really? Well, I don't like <u>cauliflower</u>.*

Ask your classmates. Share the answers.

1. Which vegetables do you eat raw? cooked?
2. Which vegetables do you put in a green salad?
3. Which vegetables are in your refrigerator right now?

69

MEAT

Beef

1. roast
2. steak
3. stewing beef
4. ground beef
5. beef ribs
6. veal cutlets
7. liver
8. tripe

Pork

9. ham
10. pork chops
11. bacon
12. sausage

Lamb

13. lamb shanks
14. leg of lamb
15. lamb chops

POULTRY

Poultry

16. chicken
17. turkey
18. duck
19. breasts
20. wings
21. legs
22. thighs
23. drumsticks
24. **raw** chicken
25. **cooked** chicken

More vocabulary

vegetarian: a person who doesn't eat meat
boneless: meat and poultry without bones
skinless: poultry without skin

Ask your classmates. Share the answers.

1. What kind of meat do you eat most often?
2. What kind of meat do you use in soups?
3. What part of the chicken do you like the most?

SEAFOOD

Special

Fish

1. trout
2. catfish
3. whole salmon
4. salmon steak
5. swordfish

6. halibut steak
7. tuna
8. cod

Shellfish

9. crab
10. lobster
11. shrimp
12. scallops
13. mussels

14. oysters
15. clams
16. **fresh** fish
17. **frozen** fish

DELI

18. white bread
19. wheat bread
20. rye bread

21. roast beef
22. corned beef
23. pastrami

24. salami
25. smoked turkey
26. American cheese

27. Swiss cheese
28. cheddar cheese
29. mozzarella cheese

Ways to order at the counter

I'd like some <u>roast beef</u>.
I'll have <u>a halibut steak</u> and some <u>shrimp</u>.
Could I get some <u>Swiss cheese</u>?

Pair practice. Make new conversations.

A: *What can I get for you?*
B: *<u>I'd like some roast beef</u>. How about a pound?*
A: *A pound of <u>roast beef</u> coming up!*

71

1. customer
2. produce section
3. scale
4. grocery clerk
5. pet food
6. aisle
7. cart
8. manager

Canned Foods

17. beans
18. soup
19. tuna

Dairy

20. margarine
21. sour cream
22. yogurt

Grocery Products

23. aluminum foil
24. plastic wrap
25. plastic storage bags

Frozen Foods

26. ice cream
27. frozen vegetables
28. frozen dinner

Ways to ask for information in a grocery store

Excuse me, where are the carrots?
Can you please tell me where to find the dog food?
Do you have any lamb chops today?

Pair practice. Make conversations.

A: *Can you please tell me where to find the dog food?*
B: *Sure. It's in aisle 1B. Do you need anything else?*
A: *Yes, where are the carrots?*

9. shopping basket	**11.** line	**13.** cashier	**15.** cash register
10. self-checkout	**12.** checkstand	**14.** bagger	**16.** bottle return

Baking Products	**Beverages**	**Snack Foods**	**Baked Goods**
29. flour	**32.** apple juice	**35.** potato chips	**38.** cookies
30. sugar	**33.** coffee	**36.** nuts	**39.** cake
31. oil	**34.** soda / pop	**37.** candy bar	**40.** bagels

Ask your classmates. Share the answers.
1. What is your favorite grocery store?
2. Do you prefer to shop alone or with friends?
3. Which foods from your country are hard to find?

Think about it. Discuss.
1. Is it better to shop every day or once a week? Why?
2. Why do grocery stores put snacks near the checkstands?
3. What's good and what's bad about small grocery stores?

73

1. bottles

 2. jars

 3. cans

 4. cartons

 5. containers

 6. boxes

 7. bags

 8. packages

 9. six-packs

 10. loaves

 11. rolls

 12. tubes

13. a bottle of water

14. a jar of jam

15. a can of beans

16. a carton of eggs

17. a container of cottage cheese

18. a box of cereal

19. a bag of flour

20. a package of cookies

21. a six-pack of soda (pop)

22. a loaf of bread

23. a roll of paper towels

24. a tube of toothpaste

Grammar Point: count and non-count

Some foods can be counted: *an apple, two apples*.
Some foods can't be counted: *some rice, some water*.
For non-count foods, count containers: *two bags of rice*.

Pair practice. Make conversations.

A: *How many <u>boxes of cereal</u> do we need?*
B: *We need <u>two boxes</u>.*

A. Measure the ingredients.

B. Weigh the food.

1 cup = 237 milliliters

C. Convert the measurements.

Liquid Measures

1 1 fl. oz.

2 1 c.

3 1 pt.

4 1 qt.

5 1 gal.

Dry Measures

6 1 tsp.

7 1 TBS.

8 1/4 c.

9 1/2 c.

10 1 c.

Weight

11

12

1. a fluid ounce of milk
2. a cup of oil
3. a pint of frozen yogurt
4. a quart of milk

5. a gallon of water
6. a teaspoon of salt
7. a tablespoon of sugar
8. a quarter cup of brown sugar

9. a half cup of raisins
10. a cup of flour
11. an ounce of cheese
12. a pound of roast beef

Equivalencies

3 tsp. = 1 TBS.	2 c. = 1 pt.
2 TBS. = 1 fl. oz.	2 pt. = 1 qt.
8 fl. oz. = 1 c.	4 qt. = 1 gal.

Volume

1 fl. oz. = 30 ml
1 c. = 237 ml
1 pt. = .47 L
1 qt. = .95 L
1 gal. = 3.79 L

Weight

1 oz. = 28.35 grams (g)
1 lb. = 453.6 g
2.205 lbs. = 1 kilogram (kg)
1 lb. = 16 oz.

Food Safety

A. **clean**

B. **separate**

C. **cook**

D. **chill**

A Clean counters!

20 SECONDS

Wash your hands!

B Use separate cutting boards for vegetables and meat!

C Cook to the right temperature!

D Refrigerate leftovers quickly!

Ways to Serve Meat and Poultry

1. fried chicken

2. barbecued / grilled ribs

3. broiled steak

4. roasted turkey

5. boiled ham

6. stir-fried beef

Ways to Serve Eggs

7. scrambled eggs

8. hardboiled eggs

9. poached eggs

10. eggs sunny-side up

11. eggs over easy

12. omelet

Role play. Make new conversations.

A: *How do you like your eggs?*
B: *I like them* scrambled. *And you?*
A: *I like them* hardboiled.

Ask your classmates. Share the answers.

1. Do you use separate cutting boards?
2. What is your favorite way to serve meat? poultry?
3. What are healthy ways of preparing meat? poultry?

Cheesy Tofu Vegetable Casserole

A. **Preheat** the oven.

B. **Grease** a baking pan.

C. **Slice** the tofu.

D. **Steam** the broccoli.

E. **Saute** the mushrooms.

F. **Spoon** sauce on top.

G. **Grate** the cheese.

H. **Bake**.

Easy Chicken Soup

I. **Cut up** the chicken.

J. **Dice** the celery.

K. **Peel** the carrots.

L. **Chop** the onions.

M. **Boil** the chicken.

N. **Add** the vegetables.

O. **Stir**.

P. **Simmer**.

Quick and Easy Cake

Q. **Break** 2 eggs into a microwave-safe bowl.

R. **Mix** the ingredients.

S. **Beat** the mixture.

T. **Microwave** for 5 minutes.

1. can opener	9. wooden spoon	17. colander	25. saucepan
2. grater	10. casserole dish	18. kitchen timer	26. cake pan
3. steamer	11. garlic press	19. spatula	27. cookie sheet
4. plastic storage container	12. carving knife	20. eggbeater	28. pie pan
5. frying pan	13. roasting pan	21. whisk	29. pot holders
6. pot	14. roasting rack	22. strainer	30. rolling pin
7. ladle	15. vegetable peeler	23. tongs	31. mixing bowl
8. double boiler	16. paring knife	24. lid	

Pair practice. Make new conversations.

A: *Please hand me the whisk.*
B: *Here's the whisk. Do you need anything else?*
A: *Yes, pass me the casserole dish.*

Use the new words.

Look at page 77. Name the kitchen utensils you see.

A: *Here's a grater.*
B: *This is a mixing bowl.*

1. hamburger
2. french fries
3. cheeseburger
4. onion rings
5. chicken sandwich
6. hot dog

7. nachos
8. taco
9. burrito
10. pizza
11. soda
12. iced tea

13. ice-cream cone
14. milkshake
15. donut
16. muffin
17. counterperson
18. straw

19. plastic utensils
20. sugar substitute
21. ketchup
22. mustard
23. mayonnaise
24. salad bar

Grammar Point: yes/no questions (do)

Do you like hamburgers? Yes, I do.
Do you like nachos? No, I don't.

Think about it. Discuss.

1. Do you think that fast food is bad for people? Why or why not?
2. What fast foods do you have in your country?
3. Do you have a favorite fast food restaurant? Which one?

79

1. bacon

2. sausage

3. hash browns

4. toast

5. English muffin

6. biscuits

7. pancakes

8. waffles

9. hot cereal

10. grilled cheese sandwich

11. pickle

12. club sandwich

13. spinach salad

14. chef's salad

15. dinner salad

16. soup

17. rolls

18. coleslaw

19. potato salad

20. pasta salad

21. fruit salad

BREAKFAST SPECIAL
Served 6 a.m. to 11 a.m.

Two egg omelet with one side

HONEY

JELLY

SYRUP

LUNCH
Served 11 a.m. to 2 p.m.
All sandwiches come with soup or salad

SIDE SALADS

SALAD DRESSINGS

Thousand Island   Ranch

Italian   Blue Cheese

Ways to order from a menu

I'd like <u>a grilled cheese sandwich</u>.

I'll have <u>a bowl of tomato soup</u>.

Could I get <u>the chef's salad</u> with <u>ranch dressing</u>?

Pair practice. Make conversations.

A: <u>I'd like a grilled cheese sandwich, please</u>.

B: Anything else for you?

A: Yes, I'll have <u>a bowl of tomato soup</u> with that.

DINNER

DESSERTS

BEVERAGES

22. roast chicken
23. mashed potatoes
24. steak
25. baked potato
26. spaghetti
27. meatballs
28. garlic bread
29. grilled fish
30. rice
31. meatloaf
32. steamed vegetables

33. layer cake
34. cheesecake
35. pie
36. mixed berries

37. coffee
38. decaf coffee
39. tea
40. herbal tea
41. cream
42. low-fat milk

Ask your classmates. Share the answers.

1. Do you prefer vegetable soup or chicken soup?
2. Do you prefer tea or coffee?
3. Which desserts on the menu do you like?

Role play. Order a dinner from the menu.

A: *Are you ready to order?*
B: *I think so. I'll have the roast chicken.*
A: *Would you also like…?*

81

1. dining room
2. hostess
3. high chair
4. booth
5. to-go box
6. patron / diner
7. menu
8. server / waiter

 A

 B

 C

D **E**

 F

 G

 H

 I

 J

A. **set** the table
B. **seat** the customer
C. **pour** the water

D. **order** from the menu
E. **take** the order
F. **serve** the meal

G. **clear** / **bus** the dishes
H. **carry** the tray
I. **pay** the check

J. **leave** a tip

More vocabulary

eat out: to go to a restaurant to eat
take out: to buy food at a restaurant and take it home to eat

Look at the pictures.
Describe what is happening.

A: *She's seating the customer.*
B: *He's taking the order.*

9. server / waitress

10. dessert tray

11. bread basket

12. busser

13. dish room

14. dishwasher

15. kitchen

16. chef

17. place setting

18. dinner plate

19. bread-and-butter plate

20. salad plate

21. soup bowl

22. water glass

23. wine glass

24. cup

25. saucer

26. napkin

27. salad fork

28. dinner fork

29. steak knife

30. knife

31. teaspoon

32. soupspoon

Pair practice. Make new conversations.

A: *Excuse me, this _spoon_ is dirty.*
B: *I'm so sorry. I'll get you a clean _spoon_ right away.*
A: *Thanks.*

Role play. Talk to a new busser.

A: *Do the _salad forks_ go on _the left_?*
B: *Yes. They go _next to the dinner forks_.*
A: *What about the…?*

1. live music	3. lemonade	5. samples	7. vendors	9. herbs
2. organic	4. sour	6. avocados	8. sweets	A. **count**

HOT FOOD

Cara's Bakery

7

8

CHIVES   DILL

PARSLEY

9

**Look at the pictures.
What do you see?**

Answer the questions.

1. How many vendors are at the market today?

2. Which vegetables are organic?

3. What are the children eating?

4. What is the woman counting? Why?

Read the story.

The Farmers' Market

On Saturdays, the Novaks go to the farmers' market. They like to visit the <u>vendors</u>. Alex Novak always goes to the hot food stand for lunch. His children love to eat the fruit <u>samples</u>. Alex's father usually buys some <u>sweets</u> and <u>lemonade</u>. The lemonade is very <u>sour</u>.

Nina Novak likes to buy <u>organic</u> <u>herbs</u> and vegetables. Today, she is buying <u>avocados</u>. The market worker <u>counts</u> eight avocados. She gives Nina one more for free.

There are other things to do at the market. The Novaks like to listen to the <u>live music</u>. Sometimes they meet friends there. The farmers' market is a great place for families on a Saturday afternoon.

Think about it.

1. What's good or bad about shopping at a farmers' market?

2. Imagine you are at the farmers' market. What will you buy?

Everyday Clothes

1. shirt

2. jeans

3. dress

4. T-shirt

5. baseball cap

6. socks

7. athletic shoes

A. **tie**

BEST OF JAZZ CONCERT

TICKETS

BEST OF JAZZ

Listen and point. Take turns.
A: *Point to the dress.*
B: *Point to the T-shirt.*
A: *Point to the baseball cap.*

Dictate to your partner. Take turns.
A: *Write dress.*
B: *Is that spelled d-r-e-s-s?*
A: *Yes. That's right.*

ONE NIGHT ONLY

8. blouse

9. handbag

10. skirt

11. suit

12. slacks / pants

13. shoes

14. sweater

B. **put on**

DOORS OPEN AT 8:00

Ways to compliment clothes

That's a pretty <u>dress</u>!
Those are great <u>shoes</u>!
I really like your <u>baseball cap</u>!

Role play. Compliment a friend.

A: *<u>That's a pretty dress</u>! <u>Green</u> is a great color on you.*
B: *Thanks! I really like your…*

Casual Clothes

1. cap

2. cardigan sweater

3. pullover sweater

4. sports shirt

5. maternity dress

6. overalls

7. knit top

8. capris

9. sandals

Work Clothes

10. uniform

11. business suit

12. tie

13. briefcase

More vocabulary

three piece suit: matching jacket, vest, and slacks
outfit: clothes that look nice together
in fashion / in style: clothes that are popular now

Describe the people. Take turns.

A: *She's wearing a maternity dress.*
B: *He's wearing a uniform.*

Formal Clothes

14. sports jacket / sports coat

15. vest

16. bow tie

17. tuxedo

18. evening gown

19. clutch bag

20. cocktail dress

21. high heels

Exercise Wear

22. sweatshirt / hoodie

23. sweatpants

24. tank top

25. shorts

Ask your classmates. Share the answers.

1. What's your favorite outfit?
2. Do you like to wear formal clothes? Why or why not?
3. Do you prefer to exercise in shorts or sweatpants?

Think about it. Discuss.

1. What jobs require formal clothes? Uniforms?
2. What's good and bad about wearing school uniforms?
3. What is your opinion of today's popular clothing?

89

1. hat	**5.** winter scarf
2. (over)coat	**6.** gloves
3. headband	**7.** headwrap
4. leather jacket	**8.** jacket

9. parka	**13.** earmuffs
10. mittens	**14.** down vest
11. ski hat	**15.** ski mask
12. leggings	**16.** down jacket

17. umbrella	**20.** rain boots
18. raincoat	**21.** trench coat
19. poncho	

22. swimming trunks	**25.** cover-up
23. straw hat	**26.** swimsuit / bathing suit
24. windbreaker	**27.** sunglasses

Grammar Point: *should*

*It's raining. You **should** take an umbrella.*
*It's snowing. You **should** wear a scarf.*
*It's sunny. You **should** wear a straw hat.*

Pair practice. Make new conversations.

A: *It's <u>snowing</u>. You should wear <u>a scarf</u>.*
B: *Don't worry. I'm wearing my <u>parka</u>.*
A: *Good, and don't forget your <u>mittens</u>.*

Unisex Underwear

1. undershirt

2. thermal undershirt

3. long underwear

Men's Underwear

4. boxer shorts

5. briefs

6. athletic supporter / jockstrap

Unisex Socks

7. ankle socks

8. crew socks

9. dress socks

Women's Socks

10. low-cut socks

11. anklets

12. knee highs

Women's Underwear

13. (bikini) panties

14. briefs / underpants

15. body shaper / girdle

16. garter belt

17. stockings

18. panty hose

19. tights

20. bra

21. camisole

22. full slip

23. half slip

Sleepwear

24. pajamas

25. nightgown

26. slippers

27. blanket sleeper

28. nightshirt

29. robe

More vocabulary

lingerie: underwear or sleepwear for women
loungewear: very casual clothing for relaxing around the home

Ask your classmates. Share the answers.

1. What kind of socks are you wearing today?
2. What kind of sleepwear do you prefer?
3. Do you wear slippers at home?

Construction Worker

Road Worker

Automotive Painter

Food Processor

1. hard hat
2. work shirt
3. tool belt

4. Hi-Visibility safety vest
5. work pants
6. steel toe boots

7. ventilation mask
8. coveralls

9. bump cap
10. safety glasses
11. apron

Manager **Salesperson**

Farmworker

Ranch Hand

12. blazer
13. tie

14. polo shirt
15. name tag

16. bandana
17. work gloves

18. cowboy hat
19. jeans

Pair practice. Make new conversations.

A: *What do <u>construction workers</u> wear to work?*
B: *They wear <u>hard hats</u> and <u>tool belts</u>.*
A: *What do <u>road workers</u> wear to work?*

Use the new words.
Look at pages 166–169. Name the workplace clothing you see.

A: *He's wearing <u>a hard hat</u>.*
B: *She's wearing <u>scrubs</u>.*

Security Guard

Emergency Worker

Counterperson

Chef

Line Cook

20. security shirt

21. badge

22. security pants

23. helmet

24. jumpsuit

25. hairnet

26. smock

27. disposable gloves

28. chef's hat

29. chef's jacket

30. waist apron

Nurse

Medical Technician

O.R.

Surgeon

Surgical Assistant

31. scrubs

32. face mask

33. lab coat

34. latex gloves

35. surgical scrub cap

36. surgical mask

37. surgical gown

38. surgical scrubs

Ask your classmates. Share the answers.

1. Which of these outfits would you like to wear?
2. Which of these items are in your closet?
3. Do you wear safety clothing at work? What kinds?

Think about it. Discuss.

1. What other jobs require helmets? disposable gloves?
2. Is it better to have a uniform or wear your own clothes at work? Why?

A. **purchase**	1. suspenders	3. salesclerk	5. display case
B. **wait** in line	2. purses / handbags	4. customer	6. belts

13. wallet	17. shoulder bag	21. sole
14. change purse / coin purse	18. backpack	22. heel
15. cell phone holder	19. tote bag	23. toe
16. (wrist)watch	20. belt buckle	24. shoelaces

More vocabulary

gift: something you give or receive from friends or family for a special occasion

present: a gift

Grammar Point: object pronouns

My **sister** loves jewelry. I'll buy **her** a necklace.
My **dad** likes belts. I'll buy **him** a belt buckle.
My **friends** love scarves. I'll buy **them** scarves.

7. shoe department	**9.** bracelets	**11.** hats	**C. try on** shoes
8. jewelry department	**10.** necklaces	**12.** scarves	**D. assist** a customer

25. high heels	**29.** oxfords	**33.** chain	**37.** clip-on earrings
26. pumps	**30.** loafers	**34.** beads	**38.** pin
27. flats	**31.** hiking boots	**35.** locket	**39.** string of pearls
28. boots	**32.** tennis shoes	**36.** pierced earrings	**40.** ring

---

Ways to talk about accessories

I need <u>a hat</u> to wear with <u>this scarf</u>.
I'd like <u>earrings</u> to go with <u>the necklace</u>.
Do you have <u>a belt</u> that would go with my <u>shoes</u>?

Role play. Talk to a salesperson.

A: *Do you have <u>boots</u> that would go with <u>this skirt</u>?*
B: *Let me see. How about <u>these brown ones</u>?*
A: *Perfect. I also need…*

Sizes

1. extra small
2. small
3. medium
4. large
5. extra large
6. one-size-fits-all

Styles

7. **crewneck** sweater

8. **V-neck** sweater

9. **turtleneck** sweater

10. **scoop neck** sweater

11. **sleeveless** shirt

12. **short-sleeved** shirt

13. **3/4-sleeved** shirt

14. **long-sleeved** shirt

15. **mini**-skirt

16. **short** skirt

17. **mid-length / calf-length** skirt

18. **long** skirt

Patterns

19. solid

20. striped

21. polka-dotted

22. plaid

23. print

24. checked

25. floral

26. paisley

Ask your classmates. Share the answers.

1. Do you prefer crewneck or V-neck sweaters?
2. Do you prefer checked or striped shirts?
3. Do you prefer short-sleeved or sleeveless shirts?

Role play. Talk to a salesperson.

A: *Excuse me. I'm looking for this <u>V-neck sweater</u> in <u>large</u>.*
B: *Here's a <u>large</u>. It's on sale for $<u>19.99</u>.*
A: *Wonderful! I'll take it. I'm also looking for…*

Comparing Clothing

27. **heavy** jacket	29. **tight** pants	31. **low** heels	33. **plain** blouse	35. **narrow** tie
28. **light** jacket	30. **loose** / **baggy** pants	32. **high** heels	34. **fancy** blouse	36. **wide** tie

Clothing Problems

37. It's **too small**.	38. It's **too big**.	39. The zipper is **broken**.	40. A button is **missing**.

41. It's **ripped** / **torn**.	42. It's **stained**.	43. It's **unraveling**.	44. It's **too expensive**.

More vocabulary

refund: money you get back when you return an item to the store
complaint: a statement that something is not right
customer service: the place customers go with their complaints

Role play. Return an item to a salesperson.

A: *Welcome to Shopmart. How may I help you?*
B: *This sweater is new, but it's unraveling.*
A: *I'm sorry. Would you like a refund?*

Making Clothes

Types of Material

1. cotton

2. linen

3. wool

4. cashmere

5. silk

6. leather

A Garment Factory

Parts of a Sewing Machine

A. **sew** by machine

B. **sew** by hand

13. sewing machine

14. sewing machine operator

15. bolt of fabric

16. rack

17. needle

18. needle plate

19. presser foot

20. feed dog / feed bar

21. bobbin

More vocabulary

fashion designer: a person who makes original clothes
natural materials: cloth made from things that grow in nature
synthetic materials: cloth made by people, such as nylon

Use the new words.
Look at pages 86–87. Name the materials you see.

A: *That's <u>denim</u>.*
B: *That's <u>leather</u>.*

98

Types of Material

7. denim

8. suede

9. lace

10. velvet

11. corduroy

12. nylon

A Fabric Store

Closures

Trim

22. pattern

23. thread

24. button

25. zipper

26. snap

27. hook and eye

28. buckle

29. hook and loop fastener

30. ribbon

31. appliqué

32. beads

33. sequins

34. fringe

Ask your classmates. Share the answers.

1. Can you sew?
2. What's your favorite type of material?
3. How many types of material are you wearing today?

Think about it. Discuss.

1. Do most people make or buy clothes in your country?
2. Is it better to make or buy clothes? Why?
3. Which materials are best for formal clothes?

99

An Alterations Shop

1. dressmaker	4. collar	7. pocket
2. dressmaker's dummy	5. waistband	8. hem
3. tailor	6. sleeve	9. cuff

Sewing Supplies

10. needle	12. (straight) pin	14. safety pin	16. pair of scissors	18. seam ripper
11. thread	13. pin cushion	15. thimble	17. tape measure	

Alterations

A. **Lengthen** the pants.

B. **Shorten** the pants.

C. **Let out** the pants.

D. **Take in** the pants.

Pair practice. Make new conversations.

A: *Would you hand me the thread?*
B: *OK. What are you going to do?*
A: *I'm going to take in these pants.*

Ask your classmates. Share the answers.

1. Is there an alterations shop near your home?
2. Do you ever go to a tailor or a dressmaker?
3. What sewing supplies do you have at home?

1. laundry
2. laundry basket
3. washer
4. dryer
5. dryer sheets

6. fabric softener
7. bleach
8. laundry detergent
9. clothesline
10. clothespin

11. hanger
12. spray starch
13. iron
14. ironing board
15. **dirty** T-shirt

16. **clean** T-shirt
17. **wet** shirt
18. **dry** shirt
19. **wrinkled** shirt
20. **ironed** shirt

A. **Sort** the laundry.

B. **Add** the detergent.

C. **Load** the washer.

D. **Clean** the lint trap.

E. **Unload** the dryer.

F. **Fold** the laundry.

G. **Iron** the clothes.

H. **Hang up** the clothes.

  wash in cold water

  no bleach

line dry

dry clean only, do not wash

Pair practice. Make new Conversations.

A: *I have to sort the laundry. Can you help?*
B: *Sure. Here's the laundry basket.*
A: *Thanks a lot!*

1. flyer
2. used clothing
3. sticker
4. folding card table
5. folding chair
6. clock radio
7. VCR

A. **bargain**

B. **browse**

Look at the pictures. What do you see?

Answer the questions.

1. What kind of used clothing do you see?
2. What information is on the flyer?
3. Why are the stickers different colors?
4. How much is the clock radio? the VCR?

📖 Read the story.

A Garage Sale

Last Sunday, I had a garage sale. At 5:00 a.m., I put up <u>flyers</u> in my neighborhood. Next, I put price <u>stickers</u> on my <u>used clothing</u>, my <u>VCR</u>, and some other old things. At 7:00 a.m., I opened my <u>folding card table</u> and <u>folding chair</u>. Then I waited.

At 7:05 a.m., my first customer arrived. She asked, "How much is the sweatshirt?"

"Two dollars," I said.

She said, "It's stained. I can give you seventy-five cents." We <u>bargained</u> for a minute and she paid $1.00.

All day people came to <u>browse</u>, bargain, and buy. At 7:00 p.m., I had $85.00.

Now I know two things: Garage sales are hard work and nobody wants to buy an old <u>clock radio</u>!

Think about it.

1. Do you like to buy things at garage sales? Why or why not?
2. Imagine you want the VCR. How will you bargain for it?

103

1. head

2. hair

3. neck

4. chest

5. back

6. nose

7. mouth

8. foot

Listen and point. Take turns.

A: *Point to the chest.*

B: *Point to the neck.*

A: *Point to the mouth.*

Dictate to your partner. Take turns.

A: *Write hair.*

B: *Did you say hair?*

A: *That's right, h-a-i-r.*

9. leg

10. toe

11. eye

12. ear

13. shoulder

14. arm

15. hand

16. finger

Grammar Point: imperatives

Please touch your right foot.
Put your hands on your feet.
Don't put your hands on your shoulders.

Pair practice. Take turns giving commands.

A: <u>Raise</u> your <u>arms</u>.
B: <u>Touch</u> your <u>feet</u>.
A: <u>Put</u> your <u>hand</u> on your <u>shoulder</u>.

105

The Face

1. chin
2. forehead
3. cheek
4. jaw

The Mouth

5. lip
6. gums
7. teeth
8. tongue

The Eye

9. eyebrow
10. eyelid
11. eyelashes

The Senses

A. **see**
B. **hear**
C. **smell**
D. **taste**
E. **touch**

The Arm, Hand, and Fingers

12. elbow
13. forearm
14. wrist
15. palm
16. thumb
17. knuckle
18. fingernail

The Leg and Foot

19. thigh
20. knee
21. shin
22. calf
23. ankle
24. heel

More vocabulary

torso: the part of the body from the shoulders to the pelvis
limbs: arms and legs
toenail: the nail on your toe

Pair practice. Make new conversations.

A: *Is your <u>arm</u> OK?*
B: *Yes, but now my <u>elbow</u> hurts.*
A: *I'm sorry to hear that.*

106

25. chest

26. breast

27. abdomen

28. shoulder blade

29. lower back

30. buttocks

31. skin

32. muscle

33. bone

THE SKELETON

34. brain

35. throat

36. artery

37. vein

38. heart

39. lung

40. liver

41. stomach

42. intestines

43. kidney

44. gallbladder

45. pancreas

46. bladder

47. skull

48. rib cage

49. spinal column

50. pelvis

107

A. take a shower

B. take a bath / **bathe**

C. use deodorant

D. put on sunscreen

1. shower cap

2. shower gel

3. soap

4. bath powder

5. deodorant / antiperspirant

6. perfume / cologne

7. sunscreen

8. sunblock

9. body lotion / moisturizer

E. wash…hair

F. rinse…hair

G. comb…hair

H. dry…hair

I. brush…hair

10. shampoo

11. conditioner

12. hair spray

13. comb

14. brush

15. pick

16. hair gel

17. curling iron

18. blow dryer

19. hair clip

20. barrette

21. bobby pins

More vocabulary

unscented: a product without perfume or scent
hypoallergenic: a product that is better for people with allergies

Think about it. Discuss.

1. Which personal hygiene products should someone use before a job interview?
2. What is the right age to start wearing makeup? Why?

J. brush…teeth

K. floss…teeth

L. gargle

M. shave

22. toothbrush

23. toothpaste

24. dental floss

25. mouthwash

26. electric shaver

27. razor

28. razorblade

29. shaving cream

30. aftershave

N. cut…nails

O. polish…nails

P. put on / apply

Q. take off / remove

Makeup

31. nail clipper

32. emery board

33. nail polish

34. eyebrow pencil

35. eye shadow

36. eyeliner

37. blush

38. lipstick

39. mascara

40. foundation

41. face powder

42. makeup remover

Symptoms and Injuries

1. headache
2. toothache
3. earache
4. stomachache
5. backache

6. sore throat
7. nasal congestion
8. fever / temperature
9. chills
10. rash

A. **cough**
B. **sneeze**
C. **feel** dizzy
D. **feel** nauseous
E. **throw up / vomit**

11. insect bite
12. bruise

13. cut
14. sunburn

15. blister
16. swollen finger

17. bloody nose
18. sprained ankle

Look at the pictures.
Describe the symptoms and injuries.

A: *He has a backache*.
B: *She has a toothache*.

Think about it. Discuss.

1. What are some common cold symptoms?
2. What do you recommend for a stomachache?
3. What is the best way to stop a bloody nose?

Common Illnesses and Childhood Diseases

1. cold

2. flu

3. ear infection

4. strep throat

5. measles

6. chicken pox

7. mumps

8. allergies

Serious Medical Conditions and Diseases

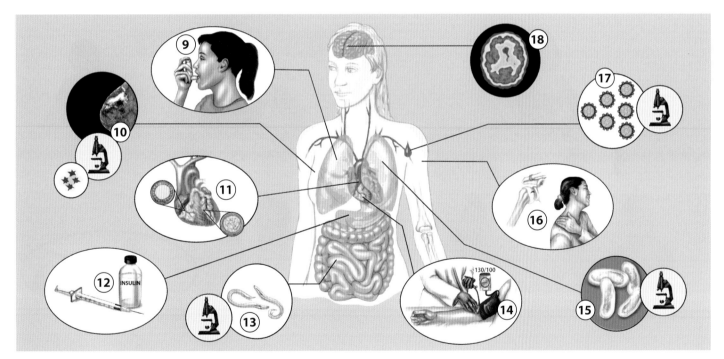

9. asthma

10. cancer

11. heart disease

12. diabetes

13. intestinal parasites

14. high blood pressure / hypertension

15. TB (tuberculosis)

16. arthritis

17. HIV (human immunodeficiency virus)

18. dementia

More vocabulary

AIDS (acquired immune deficiency syndrome): a medical condition that results from contracting the HIV virus

Alzheimer's disease: a disease that causes dementia

coronary disease: heart disease

infectious disease: a disease that is spread through air or water

influenza: flu

111

A Pharmacy

1. pharmacist
2. prescription
3. prescription medication
4. prescription label
5. prescription number
6. dosage
7. expiration date
8. warning label

Medical Warnings

A. **Take** with food or milk.

B. **Take** one hour before eating.

C. **Finish** all medication.

D. **Do not take** with dairy products.

E. **Do not drive or operate** heavy machinery.

F. **Do not drink** alcohol.

More Vocabulary

prescribe medication: to write a prescription
fill prescriptions: to prepare medication for patients
pick up a prescription: to get prescription medication

Role play. Talk to the pharmacist.

A: *Hi. I need to pick up a prescription for <u>Jones</u>.*
B: *Here's your medication, <u>Mr. Jones</u>. Take these <u>once a day with milk or food</u>.*

9. wheelchair	13. heating pad	17. vitamins
10. crutches	14. air purifier	18. over-the-counter medication
11. walker	15. hot water bottle	19. sling
12. humidifier	16. cane	20. cast

Types of Medication

21. pill	22. tablet	23. capsule	24. ointment	25. cream

Over-the-Counter Medication

26. pain reliever	28. antacid	30. throat lozenges	32. nasal spray
27. cold tablets	29. cough syrup	31. eye drops	33. inhaler

Ways to talk about medication

Use *take* for pills, tablets, capsules, and cough syrup.
Use *apply* for ointments and creams.
Use *use* for drops, nasal sprays, and inhalers.

Ask your classmates. Share the answers.

1. What pharmacy do you go to?
2. Do you ever ask the pharmacist for advice?
3. Do you take any vitamins? Which ones?

Ways to Get Well

A. **Seek** medical attention.

B. **Get** bed rest.

C. **Drink** fluids.

D. **Take** medicine.

Ways to Stay Well

E. **Stay** fit.

F. **Eat** a healthy diet.

G. **Don't smoke**.

Ms. Jones, you must stop smoking!

H. **Have** regular checkups.

I. **Get** immunized.

J. **Follow** medical advice.

More vocabulary

injection: medicine in a syringe that is put into the body

immunization / vaccination: an injection that stops serious diseases

Ask your classmates. Share the answers.

1. How do you stay fit?
2. What do you do when you're sick?
3. Which two foods are a part of your healthy diet?

114

Types of Health Problems

1. vision problems
2. hearing loss
3. pain
4. stress
5. depression

Help with Health Problems

6. optometrist
8. contact lenses
9. audiologist
10. hearing aid

7. glasses

11. physical therapy
13. talk therapy
15. support group

12. physical therapist
14. therapist

Ways to ask about health problems

Are you in pain?
Are you having vision problems?
Are you experiencing depression?

Pair practice. Make new conversations.

A: *Do you know a good optometrist?*
B: *Why? Are you having vision problems?*
A: *Yes, I might need glasses.*

Medical Emergencies

1. ambulance

2. paramedic

A. **be** unconscious

B. **be** in shock

C. **be** injured / **be** hurt

D. **have** a heart attack

E. **have** an allergic reaction

F. **get** an electric shock

G. **get** frostbite

H. **burn** (your)self

I. **drown**

J. **swallow** poison

K. **overdose** on drugs

L. **choke**

M. **bleed**

N. **can't breathe**

O. **fall**

P. **break** a bone

Grammar Point: past tense

For past tense add –ed:
burned, drowned, swallowed,
overdosed, choked

These verbs are different (irregular):

be – was, were	bleed – bled	fall – fell
have – had	can't – couldn't	
get – got	break – broke	

First Aid

1. first aid kit

2. first aid manual

3. medical emergency bracelet

Inside the Kit

4. tweezers

5. adhesive bandage

6. sterile pad

7. sterile tape

8. gauze

9. hydrogen peroxide

10. antihistamine cream

11. antibacterial ointment

12. elastic bandage

13. ice pack

14. splint

First Aid Procedures

15. stitches

16. rescue breathing

17. CPR (cardiopulmonary resuscitation)

18. Heimlich maneuver

Pair practice. Make new conversations.

A: *What do we need in the first aid kit?*

B: *We need tweezers and gauze.*

A: *I think we need sterile tape, too.*

Think about it. Discuss.

1. What are the three most important first aid items? Why?

2. Which first aid procedures should everyone know? Why?

3. What are some good places to keep a first aid kit?

Medical Care

In the Waiting Room

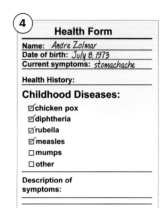

HEALTH FIRST

Name: Andre Zolmar
Group Number: 98765
Membership Number: 60756789

Health Form

Name: *Andre Zolmar*
Date of birth: *July 8, 1973*
Current symptoms: *stomachache*

Health History:

Childhood Diseases:

☑ chicken pox
☑ diphtheria
☑ rubella
☑ measles
☐ mumps
☐ other

Description of symptoms:
_____
_____

1. appointment
2. receptionist
3. health insurance card
4. health history form

In the Examining Room

5. doctor
6. patient
7. examination table
8. nurse
9. blood pressure gauge
10. stethoscope
11. thermometer
12. syringe

Medical Procedures

A. **check**…blood pressure
B. **take**…temperature

C. **listen** to…heart
D. **examine**…eyes

E. **examine**…throat
F. **draw**…blood

Grammar Point: future tense with *will* + verb

To show a future action, use *will* + verb.
The subject pronoun contraction of *will* is *-'ll.*
She *will* **draw** your blood. = She**'ll** **draw** your blood.

Role play. Talk to a medical receptionist.

A: *Will the nurse <u>examine my eyes</u>?*
B: *No, but she'll <u>draw your blood</u>.*
A: *What will the doctor do?*

Dentistry

1. dentist

2. dental assistant

3. dental hygienist

4. dental instruments

Orthodontics

5. orthodontist

6. braces

Dental Problems

7. cavity / decay

8. filling

9. crown

10. dentures

11. gum disease

12. plaque

An Office Visit

A. **clean**…teeth

B. **take** x-rays

C. **numb** the mouth

D. **drill** a tooth

E. **fill** a cavity

F. **pull** a tooth

Ask your classmates. Share the answers.

1. Do you know someone with braces? Who?
2. Do dentists make you nervous? Why or why not?
3. How often do you go to the dentist?

Role play. Talk to a dentist.

A: *I think I have a cavity.*
B: *Let me take a look.*
A: *Will I need a filling?*

119

Medical Specialists

1. internist

2. obstetrician

3. cardiologist

4. pediatrician

5. oncologist

6. radiologist

7. ophthalmologist

8. psychiatrist

Nursing Staff

9. surgical nurse

10. registered nurse (RN)

11. licensed practical nurse (LPN)

12. certified nursing assistant (CNA)

Hospital Staff

13. administrator

14. admissions clerk

15. dietician

16. orderly

More vocabulary

Gynecologists examine and treat women.
Nurse practitioners can give medical exams.
Nurse midwives deliver babies.

Chiropractors move the spine to improve health.
Orthopedists treat bone and joint problems.

A Hospital Room

Lab

17. volunteer
18. patient
19. hospital gown
20. medication

21. bed table
22. hospital bed
23. bed pan
24. medical chart

25. IV (intravenous drip)
26. vital signs monitor
27. bed control
28. call button

29. phlebotomist
30. blood work / blood test
31. medical waste disposal

Emergency Room Entrance

Operating Room

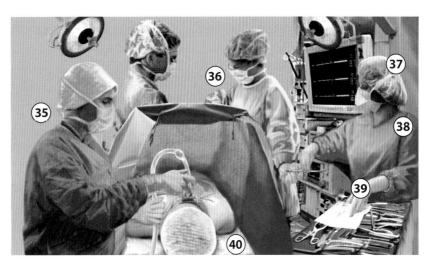

32. emergency medical technician (EMT)
33. stretcher / gurney
34. ambulance

35. anesthesiologist
36. surgeon

37. surgical cap
38. surgical gown

39. surgical gloves
40. operating table

Dictate to your partner. Take turns.

A: *Write this sentence. She's a volunteer.*
B: *She's a what?*
A: *Volunteer. That's v-o-l-u-n-t-e-e-r.*

Role play. Ask about a doctor.

A: *I need to find a good surgeon.*
B: *Dr. Jones is a great surgeon. You should call him.*
A: *I will! Please give me his number.*

FADOOL HEALTH CLINIC

HEALTH FAIR
SATURDAY 9-4

GOOD FOODS MARKET

Vitamins

TREATMENT
$5.00

FREE
EYE
EXAM

MEDICAL
SCREENING
$2

HATHA
2-3

FUN and FIT
10-11

| 1. low-cost exam | 3. booth | 5. aerobic exercise | 7. sugar-free | A. **check** ... pulse |
| 2. acupuncture | 4. yoga | 6. demonstration | 8. nutrition label | B. **give** a lecture |

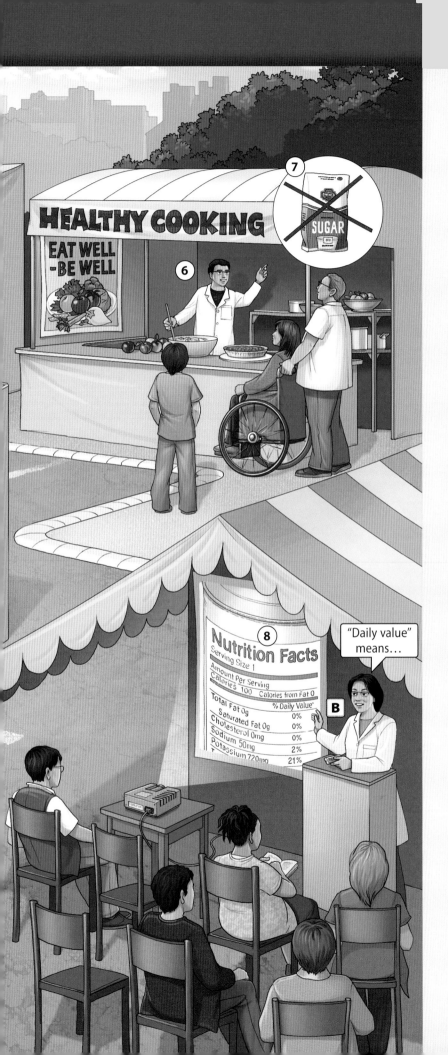

**Look at the picture.
What do you see?**

Answer the questions.

1. How many different booths are there at the health fair?

2. What kinds of exams and treatments can you get at the fair?

3. What kinds of lectures and demonstrations are there?

4. How much is an acupuncture treatment? a medical screening?

📖 Read the story.

A Health Fair

Once a month the Fadool Health Clinic has a health fair. You can get a low-cost medical exam at one booth. The nurses check your blood pressure and check your pulse. At another booth you can get a free eye exam. And an acupuncture treatment is only $5.00.

You can learn a lot at the fair. This month a doctor is giving a lecture on nutrition labels. There is also a demonstration on sugar-free cooking. You can learn to do aerobic exercise and yoga, too.

Do you want to get healthy and stay healthy? Then come to the Fadool Clinic Health Fair!

Think about it.

1. Which booths at this fair look interesting to you? Why?

2. Do you read nutrition labels? Why or why not?

Downtown

1. parking garage

2. office building

3. hotel

4. Department of Motor Vehicles

5. bank

6. police station

7. bus station

8. city hall

Listen and point. Take turns.

A: *Point to the bank.*
B: *Point to the hotel.*
A: *Point to the restaurant.*

Dictate to your partner. Take turns.

A: *Write bank.*
B: *Is that spelled b-a-n-k?*
A: *Yes, that's right.*

9. hospital

10. gas station

11. post office

12. fire station

13. courthouse

14. restaurant

15. library

Grammar Point: *in* and *at* with locations

Use *in* when you are inside the building. *I am in (inside) the bank.* Use *at* to describe your general location. *I am at the bank.*

Pair practice. Make new conversations.

A: *I'm in the <u>bank</u>. Where are you?*

B: *I'm at the <u>bank</u>, too, but I'm outside.*

A: *OK. I'll meet you there.*

125

1. stadium
2. construction site
3. factory
4. car dealership

5. mosque
6. movie theater
7. shopping mall
8. furniture store

9. school
10. gym
11. coffee shop
12. motel

Ways to state your destination using *to* and *to the*

Use *to* for schools, churches, and synagogues.
*I'm going **to** <u>school</u>.*
Use ***to the*** for all other locations. *I have to go **to the** <u>bakery</u>.*

Pair practice. Make new conversations.

A: *Where are you going today?*
B: *I'm going to <u>school</u>. How about you?*
A: *I have to go to the <u>bakery</u>.*

13. skyscraper / high-rise

14. church

15. cemetery

16. synagogue

17. community college

18. supermarket

19. bakery

20. home improvement store

21. office supply store

22. garbage truck

23. theater

24. convention center

Ways to give locations

The mall is on 2nd Street.
The mall is on the corner of 2nd and Elm.
The mall is next to the movie theater.

Ask your classmates. Share the answers.

1. Where's your favorite coffee shop?
2. Where's your favorite supermarket?
3. Where's your favorite movie theater?

127

1. laundromat	7. corner	13. mailbox
2. dry cleaners	8. traffic light	14. pedestrian
3. convenience store	9. bus	15. crosswalk
4. pharmacy	10. fast food restaurant	A. **cross** the street
5. parking space	11. drive-thru window	B. **wait for** the light
6. handicapped parking	12. newsstand	C. **jaywalk**

Pair practice. Make new conversations.

A: *I have a lot of errands to do today.*
B: *Me, too. First, I'm going to the laundromat.*
A: *I'll see you there after I stop at the copy center.*

Think about it. Discuss.

1. Which businesses are good to have in a neighborhood? Why?
2. Would you like to own a small business? If yes, what kind? If no, why not?

16. bus stop	**22.** bike	**28.** cart
17. donut shop	**23.** pay phone	**29.** street vendor
18. copy center	**24.** sidewalk	**30.** childcare center
19. barbershop	**25.** parking meter	**D. ride** a bike
20. video store	**26.** street sign	**E. park** the car
21. curb	**27.** fire hydrant	**F. walk** a dog

More vocabulary

neighborhood: the area close to your home
do errands: to make a short trip from your home to buy or pick up things

Ask your classmates. Share the answers.

1. What errands do you do every week?
2. What stores do you go to in your neighborhood?
3. What things can you buy from a street vendor?

129

1. music store
2. jewelry store
3. nail salon
4. bookstore

5. toy store
6. pet store
7. card store
8. florist

9. optician
10. shoe store
11. play area
12. guest services

More vocabulary

beauty shop: hair salon
men's store: men's clothing store
gift shop: a store that sells t-shirts, mugs, and other small gifts

Pair practice. Make new conversations.

A: *Where is the florist?*
B: *It's on the first floor, next to the optician.*

13. department store

14. travel agency

15. food court

16. ice cream shop

17. candy store

18. hair salon

19. maternity store

20. electronics store

21. elevator

22. cell phone kiosk

23. escalator

24. directory

Ways to talk about plans

Let's go to the <u>card store</u>.
I have to go to the <u>card store</u>.
I want to go to the <u>card store</u>.

Role play. Talk to a friend at the mall.

A: *Let's go to the <u>card store</u>. I need to buy <u>a card</u> for Maggie's birthday.*
B: *OK, but can we go to the <u>shoe store</u> next?*

131

1. teller	3. deposit
2. customer	4. deposit slip

5. security guard	7. safety deposit box
6. vault	8. valuables

Opening an Account

9. account manager	12. check book	15. ATM card
10. passbook	13. check	16. bank statement
11. savings account number	14. checking account number	17. balance

A. **Cash** a check.

B. **Make** a deposit.

C. **Bank** online.

The ATM (Automated Teller Machine)

D. **Insert** your ATM card.

E. **Enter** your PIN.*

F. **Withdraw** cash.

G. **Remove** your card.

*PIN = personal identification number

A. get a library card

B. look for a book

C. check out a book

D. return a book

E. pay a late fine

1. library clerk
2. circulation desk
3. library patron

4. periodicals
5. magazine
6. newspaper

7. headline
8. atlas
9. reference librarian

10. self-checkout
11. online catalog
12. picture book

13. biography
14. title

15. author
16. novel

17. audiobook
18. videocassette

19. DVD

The Post Office

1. Priority Mail®

2. Express Mail®

3. media mail

4. Certified Mail™

5. airmail

6. ground post / parcel post

13. letter

14. envelope

15. greeting card

16. post card

17. package

18. book of stamps

19. postal forms

20. letter carrier

21. return address

22. mailing address

23. stamp

24. postmark

21 Sonya Enriquez
258 Quentin Avenue
Los Angeles, CA 90068-141

22 Cindy Lin
807 Glenn Drive
Charlotte, NC 28201

Ways to talk about sending mail

This letter has to *get there tomorrow*. (Express Mail®)
This letter has to *arrive in two days*. (Priority Mail®)
This letter can go in *regular mail*. (First Class)

Pair practice. Make new conversations.

A: Hi. *This letter has to get there tomorrow*.
B: You can send it by *Express Mail*®.
A: OK. I need *a book of stamps*, too.

7. postal clerk

8. scale

9. post office box (PO box)

10. automated postal center (APC)

11. stamp machine

12. mailbox

Sending a Card

A. Write a note in a card.

B. Address the envelope.

C. Put on a stamp.

D. Mail the card.

E. Deliver the card.

F. Receive the card.

G. Read the card.

H. Write back.

More vocabulary

overnight / next day mail: Express Mail®
postage: the cost to send mail
junk mail: mail you don't want

Think about it. Discuss.

1. What kind of mail do you send overnight?
2. Do you want to be a letter carrier? Why or why not?
3. Do you get junk mail? What do you do with it?

Department of Motor Vehicles (DMV)

1. DMV handbook
2. testing area
3. DMV clerk
4. photo
5. fingerprint
6. vision exam
7. window

8. proof of insurance
9. driver's license
10. expiration date
11. driver's license number
12. license plate
13. registration sticker / tag

More vocabulary

expire: a license is no good, or **expires**, after the expiration date
renew a license: to apply to keep a license before it expires
vanity plate: a more expensive, personal license plate

Ask your classmates. Share the answers.

1. How far is the DMV from your home?
2. Do you have a driver's license? If yes, when does it expire? If not, do you want one?

Getting Your First License

A. **Study** the handbook.

B. **Take** a driver education course.*

C. **Show** your identification.

D. **Pay** the application fee.

E. **Take** a written test.

F. **Get** a learner's permit.

G. **Take** a driver's training course.*

H. **Pass** a driving test.

I. **Get** your license.

*Note: This is not required for drivers 18 and older.

Ways to request more information

What do I do next?
What's the next step?
Where do I go from here?

Role play. Talk to a DMV clerk.

A: *I want to apply for <u>a driver's license</u>.*
B: *Did you <u>study the handbook</u>?*
A: *Yes, I did. <u>What do I do next</u>?*

Government and Military Service

Federal Government

Legislative Branch

1. U.S. Capitol
2. Congress
3. House of Representatives
4. congressperson
5. Senate
6. senator

Executive Branch

7. White House
8. president
9. vice president
10. Cabinet

Judicial Branch

11. Supreme Court
12. justices
13. chief justice

The Military

14. Army
15. Navy
16. Air Force
17. Marines
18. Coast Guard
19. National Guard

State Government

City Government

20. governor

21. lieutenant governor

22. state capital

23. Legislature

24. assemblyperson

25. state senator

26. mayor

27. city council

28. councilperson

An Election

A. **run for** office

29. political campaign

B. **debate**

30. opponent

C. **get elected**

31. election results

D. **serve**

32. elected official

More vocabulary

term: the period of time an elected official serves
political party: a group of people with the same political goals

Think about it. Discuss.

1. Should everyone have to serve in the military? Why or why not?
2. Would you prefer to run for city council or mayor? Why?

139

Responsibilities

A. **vote**

B. **pay** taxes

C. **obey** the law

D. **register** with Selective Service*

E. **serve** on a jury

F. **be** informed

Citizenship Requirements

G. **be** 18 or older

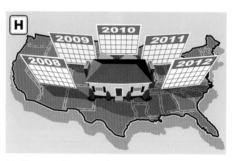

H. **live** in the U.S. for 5 years

I. **take** a citizenship test

Rights

1. peaceful assembly

2. free speech

3. freedom of religion

4. freedom of the press

5. fair trial

*Note: All males 18 to 26 who live in the U.S. are required to register with Selective Service.

A. **arrest** a suspect

1. police officer
2. handcuffs

B. **hire** a lawyer / **hire** an attorney

3. guard
4. defense attorney

C. **appear** in court

5. defendant
6. judge

D. **stand** trial

7. courtroom

8. jury
9. evidence

10. prosecuting attorney
11. witness

12. court reporter
13. bailiff

E. **convict** the defendant

14. verdict*

F. **sentence** the defendant

G. **go** to jail / **go** to prison

15. convict / prisoner

H. **be** released

*Note: There are two possible verdicts, "guilty" and "not guilty."

Look at the pictures.
Describe what happened.

A: *The police officer arrested a suspect*.
B: *He put handcuffs on him*.

Think about it. Discuss.

1. Would you want to serve on a jury? Why or why not?
2. Look at the crimes on page 142. What sentence would you give for each crime? Why?

1. vandalism

2. burglary

3. assault

4. gang violence

5. drunk driving

6. illegal drugs

7. arson

8. shoplifting

9. identity theft

10. victim

Town Bank Online
Town Bank Customer:
Jane Montes
Withdrawal Amount:
$ 10,000.00

Jane Montes
Town Bank Statement
Account
Balance:
$0.00

11. mugging

12. murder

13. gun

More vocabulary

steal: to take money or things from someone illegally
commit a crime: to do something illegal
criminal: someone who does something illegal

Think about it. Discuss.

1. Is there too much crime on TV or in the movies? Explain.
2. How can communities help stop crime?

A. **Walk** with a friend.

B. **Stay** on well-lit streets.

C. **Conceal** your PIN number.

D. **Protect** your purse or wallet.

E. **Lock** your doors.

F. Don't **open** your door to strangers.

G. Don't **drink** and **drive**.

H. **Shop** on secure websites.

I. **Be** aware of your surroundings.

J. **Report** suspicious packages.

K. **Report** crimes to the police.

L. **Join** a Neighborhood Watch.

More vocabulary

sober: not drunk
designated drivers: sober drivers who drive drunk people home safely

Ask your classmates. Share the answers.

1. Do you feel safe in your neighborhood?
2. Look at the pictures. Which of these things do you do?
3. What other things do you do to stay safe?

143

1. lost child

2. car accident

3. airplane crash

4. explosion

5. earthquake

6. mudslide

7. forest fire

8. fire

9. firefighter

10. fire truck

Ways to report an emergency

First, give your name. *My name is <u>Tim Johnson</u>.*
Then, state the emergency and give the address.
There was <u>a car accident</u> at <u>219 Elm Street</u>.

Role play. Call 911.

A: *911 Emergency Operator.*
B: *My name is <u>Lisa Diaz</u>. There is <u>a fire</u> at <u>323 Oak Street</u>.
Please hurry!*

11. drought

12. famine

13. blizzard

14. hurricane

15. tornado

16. volcanic eruption

17. tidal wave / tsunami

18. avalanche

19. flood

20. search and rescue team

Ask your classmates. Share the answers.

1. Which natural disaster worries you the most?
2. Which natural disaster worries you the least?
3. Which disasters are common in your local area?

Think about it. Discuss.

1. What organizations can help you in an emergency?
2. What are some ways to prepare for natural disasters?
3. Where would you go in an emergency?

145

Before an Emergency

A. Plan for an emergency.

1. meeting place

2. out-of-state contact

3. escape route

4. gas shut-off valve

5. evacuation route

B. Make a disaster kit.

6. warm clothes

7. blankets

8. can opener

9. canned food

10. packaged food

11. bottled water

12. moist towelettes

13. toilet paper

14. flashlight

15. batteries

16. matches

17. cash and coins

18. first aid kit

19. copies of ID and credit cards

20. copies of important papers

Pair practice. Make new conversations.

A: *What do we need for our disaster kit?*
B: *We need blankets and matches.*
A: *I think we also need batteries.*

Ask your classmates. Share the answers.

1. Who would you call first after an emergency?
2. Do you have escape and evacuation routes planned?
3. Are you a calm person in case of an emergency?

During an Emergency

C. **Watch** the weather.

D. **Pay attention** to warnings.

E. **Remain** calm.

F. **Follow** directions.

G. **Help** people with disabilities.

H. **Seek** shelter.

I. **Stay away** from windows.

J. **Take** cover.

K. **Evacuate** the area.

After an Emergency

L. **Call** out-of-state contacts.

M. **Clean up** debris.

N. **Inspect** utilities.

Ways to say you're OK	Ways to say you need help	Role play. Prepare for an emergency.
I'm fine.	*We need help.*	A: *They just issued <u>a hurricane</u> warning.*
We're OK here.	*Someone is hurt.*	B: *OK. We need to stay calm and follow directions.*
Everything's under control.	*I'm injured. Please get help.*	A: *What do we need to do first?*

147

1. graffiti
2. litter
3. streetlight
4. hardware store
5. petition
A. **give** a speech
B. **applaud**
C. **change**

Look at the pictures. What do you see?

Answer the questions.

1. What were the problems on Main Street?

2. What was the petition for?

3. Why did the city council applaud?

4. How did the people change the street?

📖 **Read the story.**

Community Cleanup

Marta Lopez has a donut shop on Main Street. One day she looked at her street and was very upset. She saw graffiti on her donut shop and the other stores. Litter was everywhere. All the streetlights were broken. Marta wanted to fix the lights and clean up the street.

Marta started a petition about the streetlights. Five hundred people signed it. Then she gave a speech to the city council. The council members voted to repair the streetlights. Everyone applauded. Marta was happy, but her work wasn't finished.

Next, Marta asked for volunteers to clean up Main Street. The hardware store manager gave the volunteers free paint. Marta gave them free donuts and coffee. The volunteers painted and cleaned. They changed Main Street. Now Main Street is beautiful and Marta is proud.

Think about it.

1. What are some problems in your community? How can people help?

2. Imagine you are Marta. What do you say in your speech to the city council?

1. car

2. passenger

3. taxi

4. motorcycle

5. street

6. truck

7. train

8. (air)plane

Listen and point. Take turns.

A: *Point to the motorcycle.*

B: *Point to the truck.*

A: *Point to the train.*

Dictate to your partner. Take turns.

A: *Write motorcycle.*

B: *Could you repeat that for me?*

A: *Motorcycle. M-o-t-o-r-c-y-c-l-e.*

9. helicopter

10. airport

11. subway station

12. subway

13. bus stop

14. bus

15. bicycle

Ways to talk about using transportation

Use **take** for buses, trains, subways, taxis, planes, and helicopters. Use **drive** for cars and trucks. Use **ride** for bicycles and motorcycles.

Pair practice. Make new conversations.

A: *How do you get to school?*
B: *I take the bus. How about you?*
A: *I ride a bicycle to school.*

A Bus Stop

BUS 10 Northbound		
Main	Elm	Oak
6:00	6:10	6:13
6:30	6:40	6:43
7:00	7:10	7:13
7:30	7:40	7:43

New York City Transit
MTA Transfer
◄ Going your way

1. bus route
2. fare
3. rider
4. schedule
5. transfer

A Subway Station

MTA RED LINE
1 FARE
NORTH HOLLYWOOD

MetroCard
◄─── Insert this way/This side facing you

6. subway car
7. platform
8. turnstile
9. vending machine
10. token
11. fare card

A Train Station

HART DAVIS/DAMON
From
DOVER, NH
To
BOSTON NRTH STA, MA
Carrier Train Date
2V 684 17FEB03
Accom Space/Car
2V BUSINESS CL
Form of Payment
AP XXXX0456791 Ax

Fresno
Los Angeles

Fresno
Los Angeles

12. ticket window
13. conductor
14. track
15. ticket
16. one-way trip
17. round trip

Airport Transportation

TAXIS
TAXI
J&J Hotel

1036081
22.00

18. taxi stand
19. shuttle
20. town car
21. taxi driver
22. taxi license
23. meter

More vocabulary

hail a taxi: to raise your hand to get a taxi
miss the bus: to get to the bus stop after the bus leaves

Ask your classmates. Share the answers.

1. Is there a subway system in your city?
2. Do you ever take taxis? When?
3. Do you ever take the bus? Where?

A. **go under** the bridge   B. **go over** the bridge

C. **walk up** the steps   D. **walk down** the steps

E. **get into** the taxi   F. **get out of** the taxi   G. **run across** the street   H. **run around** the corner

I. **get on** the highway   J. **get off** the highway   K. **drive through** the tunnel

---

Grammar Point: *into, out of, on, off*

Use ***get into*** for taxis and cars.
Use ***get on*** for buses, trains, planes, and highways.

Use ***get out of*** for taxis and cars.
Use ***get off*** for buses, trains, planes, and highways.

1. stop

2. do not enter / wrong way **3.** one way **4.** speed limit

5. U-turn OK

6. no outlet / dead end

7. right turn only

8. no left turn

9. yield

10. merge

11. no parking

12. handicapped parking

13. pedestrian crossing

14. railroad crossing

15. school crossing

16. road work

17. U.S. route / highway marker

18. hospital

Pair practice. Make new conversations.

A: *Watch out! The sign says <u>no left turn</u>.*
B: *Sorry, I was looking at the <u>stop</u> sign.*
A: *That's OK. Just be careful!*

Ask your classmates. Share the answers.

1. How many traffic signs are on your street?
2. What's the speed limit on your street?
3. What traffic signs are the same in your native country?

Directions

A. Go straight on Elm Street.

B. Turn right on Pine Street.

C. Turn left on Oak Street.

D. Stop at the corner.

E. Go past Main Street.

F. Go one block to First Street.

Maps

1. north
2. west
3. south
4. east
5. symbol
6. key
7. scale
8. street
9. highway
10. river
11. GPS (global positioning system)
12. Internet map

Role play. Ask for directions.

A: *I'm lost. I need to get to Elm and Pine.*

B: *Go straight on Oak and make a right on Pine.*

A: *Thanks so much.*

Ask your classmates. Share the answers.

1. How often do you use Internet maps? GPS? paper maps?

2. What was the last map you used? Why?

1. 4-door car / sedan
2. 2-door car / coupe
3. hybrid
4. sports car

5. convertible
6. station wagon
7. SUV (sport–utility vehicle)
8. minivan

9. camper
10. RV (recreational vehicle)
11. limousine / limo

12. pickup truck
13. cargo van

14. tow truck
15. tractor trailer / semi

16. cab
17. trailer

18. moving van
19. dump truck

20. tank truck
21. school bus

Pair practice. Make new conversations.

A: *I have a new car!*
B: *Did you get a hybrid?*
A: *Yes, but I really wanted a sports car.*

More vocabulary

make: the name of the company that makes the car
model: the style of the car

Buying a Used Car

A. **Look at** car ads.

B. **Ask** the seller about the car.

C. **Take** the car to a mechanic.

D. **Negotiate** a price.

E. **Get** the title from the seller.

F. **Register** the car.

Taking Care of Your Car

G. **Fill** the tank with gas.

H. **Check** the oil.

I. **Put in** coolant.

J. **Go** for a smog check.*

K. **Replace** the windshield wipers.

L. **Fill** the tires with air.

*smog check = emissions test

Ways to request service

Please check the oil.
Could you fill the tank?
Put in coolant, please.

Think about it. Discuss.

1. What's good and bad about a used car?
2. Do you like to negotiate car prices? Why?
3. Do you know any good mechanics? Why are they good?

157

At the Dealer

At the Mechanic

1. windshield
2. windshield wipers
3. sideview mirror
4. hood
5. tire
6. turn signal
7. headlight
8. bumper

9. hubcap / wheel cover
10. gas tank
11. trunk
12. license plate
13. tail light
14. brake light
15. tail pipe
16. muffler

Under the Hood

Inside the Trunk

17. fuel injection system
18. engine
19. radiator
20. battery

21. jumper cables
22. lug wrench
23. spare tire
24. jack

The Dashboard and Instrument Panel

25. door lock	**30.** temperature gauge	**35.** rearview mirror	**40.** heater
26. steering wheel	**31.** gas gauge	**36.** hazard lights	**41.** defroster
27. speedometer	**32.** horn	**37.** radio	**42.** power outlet
28. odometer	**33.** ignition	**38.** CD player	**43.** air bag
29. oil gauge	**34.** turn signal	**39.** air conditioner	**44.** glove compartment

An Automatic Transmission

A Manual Transmission

Inside the Car

45. brake pedal	**47.** gear shift	**49.** clutch	**51.** front seat	**53.** child safety seat
46. gas pedal / accelerator	**48.** hand brake	**50.** stick shift	**52.** seat belt	**54.** backseat

In the Airline Terminal

At the Security Checkpoint

1. skycap

2. check-in kiosk

3. ticket agent

4. screening area

5. TSA* agent / security screener

6. bin

Taking a Flight

A. **Check in** electronically.

B. **Check** your bags.

C. **Show** your boarding pass and ID.

D. **Go through** security.

E. **Board** the plane.

F. **Find** your seat.

G. **Stow** your carry-on bag.

H. **Fasten** your seat belt.

I. **Turn off** your cell phone.

J. **Take off**. / **Leave**.

K. **Land**. / **Arrive**.

L. **Claim** your baggage.

* Transportation Security Administration

At the Gate

7. arrival and departure monitors

8. gate

9. boarding area

On the Airplane

10. cockpit

11. pilot

12. flight attendant

13. overhead compartment

14. emergency exit

15. passenger

At Customs

16. declaration form

17. customs officer

18. luggage / bag

19. e-ticket

20. boarding pass

21. tray table

22. turbulence

23. baggage carousel

24. oxygen mask

25. life vest

26. emergency card

27. reclined seat

28. upright seat

29. on-time

30. delayed flight

More vocabulary

departure time: the time the plane takes off
arrival time: the time the plane lands
direct flight: a trip with no stops

Pair practice. Make new conversations.

A: *Excuse me. Where do I <u>check in</u>?*
B: *At the <u>check-in kiosk</u>.*
A: *Thanks.*

Seattle

SPEED LIMIT 65

AUTO CLUB
Joe Gomez
429 014 012345678 9

1. starting point	4. auto club card	B. **get** lost	E. **run out** of gas
2. scenery	5. destination	C. **get** a speeding ticket	F. **have** a flat tire
3. gas station attendant	A. **pack**	D. **break down**	

Look at the pictures. What do you see?

Answer the questions.

1. What are the young men's starting point and destination?

2. What do they see on their trip?

3. What kinds of problems do they have?

📖 Read the story.

A Road Trip

On July 7th Joe and Rob <u>packed</u> their bags for a road trip. Their <u>starting point</u> was Seattle. Their <u>destination</u> was New York City.

The young men saw beautiful <u>scenery</u> on their trip. But there were also problems. They <u>got lost</u>. Then, a <u>gas station attendant</u> gave them bad directions. Next, they <u>got a speeding ticket</u>. Joe was very upset. After that, their car <u>broke down</u>. Joe called a tow truck and used his <u>auto club card</u>.

The end of their trip was difficult, too. They <u>ran out of gas</u> and then they had a <u>flat tire</u>.

After 7,000 miles of problems, Joe and Rob arrived in New York City. They were happy, but tired. Next time, they're going to take the train.

Think about it.

1. What is the best way to travel across the U.S.? by car? by plane? by train? Why?

2. Imagine your car breaks down on the road. Who can you call? What can you do?

The Workplace

1. entrance

2. customer

3. office

4. employer / boss

5. receptionist

6. safety regulations

IRINA'S COMPUTER SERVICE

6 OSHA

HAZARDS

SPILLS

CALL 911

SAFETY FIRST

COMPUTER NEWS

Irina Sarkov Owner

Listen and point. Take turns.

A: Point to <u>the front entrance</u>.

B: Point to <u>the receptionist</u>.

A: Point to <u>the time clock</u>.

Dictate to your partner. Take turns.

A: *Can you spell <u>employer</u>?*

B: *I'm not sure. Is it <u>e-m-p-l-o-y-e-r</u>?*

A: *Yes, that's right.*

7. time clock
8. supervisor
9. employee
10. payroll clerk
11. pay stub
12. wages
13. deductions
14. paycheck

Ways to talk about wages

I **earn** $250 a week.
He **makes** $7 an hour.
I'm **paid** $1,000 a month.

Role play. Talk to an employer.

A: *Is everything correct on your paycheck?*
B: *No, it isn't. I make $250 a week, not $200.*
A: *Let's talk to the payroll clerk. Where is she?*

165

1. accountant

2. actor

3. administrative assistant

4. appliance repair person

5. architect

6. artist

7. assembler

8. auto mechanic

9. babysitter

10. baker

11. business owner

12. businessperson

13. butcher

14. carpenter

15. cashier

16. childcare worker

Ways to ask about someone's job

What's her job?
What does he do?
What kind of work do they do?

Pair practice. Make new conversations.

A: *What kind of work <u>does she</u> do?*
B: <u>*She's an accountant*</u>*. What <u>do they</u> do?*
A: <u>*They're actors*</u>*.*

17. commercial fisher

18. computer software engineer

19. computer technician

We have that shirt in red.
20. customer service representative

21. delivery person

22. dental assistant

23. dockworker

24. electronics repair person

25. engineer

26. firefighter

27. florist

28. gardener

29. garment worker

30. graphic designer

31. hairdresser / hair stylist

32. home health care aide

Ways to talk about jobs and occupations

Sue's a garment worker. She works in a factory.
Tom's an engineer. He works for a large company.
Ann's a dental assistant. She works with a dentist.

Role play. Talk about a friend's new job.

A: *Does your friend like his new job?*
B: *Yes, he does. He's a graphic designer.*
A: *Does he work in an office?*

167

33. homemaker

34. housekeeper

你好

He says, "Hi."

35. interpreter / translator

36. lawyer

37. machine operator

38. manicurist

39. medical records technician

40. messenger / courier

41. model

42. mover

43. musician

44. nurse

45. occupational therapist

46. (house) painter

47. physician assistant

48. police officer

Grammar Point: past tense of be

I **was** a machine operator for 5 years.
She **was** a nurse for a year.
They **were** movers from 2003–2007.

Pair practice. Make new conversations.

A: *What was your first job?*
B: *I was a musician. How about you?*
A: *I was a messenger for a small company.*

49. postal worker

50. printer

51. receptionist

52. reporter

53. retail clerk

54. sanitation worker

55. security guard

56. server

Here are some programs that will help you.

57. social worker

58. soldier

59. stock clerk

Hello. I'm calling with a very special offer.

60. telemarketer

61. truck driver

62. veterinarian

63. welder

64. writer / author

Ask your classmates. Share the answers.

1. Which of these jobs could you do now?
2. What is one job you don't want to have?
3. Which jobs do you want to have?

Think about it. Discuss.

1. Which jobs need special training?
2. What kind of person makes a good interpreter? A good nurse? A good reporter? Why?

A. assemble components

B. assist medical patients

C. cook

D. do manual labor

E. drive a truck

F. fly a plane

G. make furniture

H. operate heavy machinery

I. program computers

J. repair appliances

K. sell cars

L. sew clothes

4% interest of 5K = x

M. solve math problems

ПРИВЕТ

N. speak another language

O. supervise people

P. take care of children

Q. teach

R. type

S. use a cash register

T. wait on customers

Grammar Point: can, can't

*I am a chef. I **can** cook.*
*I'm not a pilot. I **can't** fly a plane.*
*I **can't** speak French, but I **can** speak Spanish.*

Role play. Talk to a job counselor.

A: *Tell me about your skills. Can you <u>type</u>?*
B: <u>*No, I can't*</u>*, but I <u>can use a cash register</u>.*
A: *OK. What other skills do you have?*

Customers need better service…

Office Skills

A. **type** a letter

B. **enter** data

C. **transcribe** notes

D. **make** copies

E. **collate** papers

F. **staple**

G. **fax** a document

H. **scan** a document

I. **print** a document

Let's meet at 2:00.

Sure.

Dear Mr. Smith…

J. **schedule** a meeting

K. **take** dictation

L. **organize** materials

Hello. ABC Company. How may I help you?

Please hold.

Mr. Perez, I'm transferring you.

Telephone Skills

M. **greet** the caller

N. **put** the caller on hold

O. **transfer** the call

Hello. This is Sue Jones. Please call me.

Message Pad
Call From: Ana Puerta
Tel: 555-1234
Message: Please Call

This is Lee Tran. Please call me back.

P. **leave** a message

Q. **take** a message

R. **check** messages

Career Path

1. entry-level job

2. training

3. new job

4. promotion

Types of Job Training

5. vocational training

6. internship

7. on-the-job training

8. online course

Planning a Career

9. resource center

10. career counselor

11. interest inventory

12. skill inventory

13. job fair

14. recruiter

Ways to talk about job training

I'm looking into an online course.
I'm interested in on-the-job training.
I want to sign up for an internship.

Ask your classmates. Share the answers.

1. What kind of job training are you interested in?
2. Would your rather learn English in an online course or in a classroom?

A. talk to friends / **network**

B. look in the classifieds

C. look for help wanted signs

D. check Internet job sites

E. go to an employment agency

F. write a resume

G. write a cover letter

H. send in your resume
and cover letter

I. set up an interview

J. fill out an application

K. go on an interview

L. get hired

A. **Prepare** for the interview.

B. **Dress** appropriately.

C. **Be** neat.

D. **Bring** your resume and ID.

E. **Don't be** late.

F. **Be** on time.

G. **Turn off** your cell phone.

H. **Greet** the interviewer.

I. **Shake** hands.

J. **Make** eye contact.

K. **Listen** carefully.

L. **Talk** about your experience.

M. **Ask** questions.

N. **Thank** the interviewer.

O. **Write** a thank-you note.

More vocabulary

benefits: health insurance, vacation pay, or other things the employer can offer an employee
inquire about benefits: ask about benefits

Think about it. Discuss.

1. How can you prepare for an interview?
2. Why is it important to make eye contact?
3. What kinds of questions should you ask?

1. factory owner	5. parts	9. conveyer belt	13. pallet
2. designer	6. assembly line	10. order puller	14. shipping clerk
3. factory worker	7. warehouse	11. hand truck	15. loading dock
4. line supervisor	8. packer	12. forklift	

A. **design**

B. **manufacture**

C. **assemble**

D. **ship**

1. gardening crew
2. leaf blower
3. wheelbarrow
4. gardening crew leader

5. landscape designer
6. lawn mower
7. shovel
8. rake

9. pruning shears
10. trowel
11. hedge clippers
12. weed whacker / weed eater

A. **mow** the lawn

B. **trim** the hedges

C. **rake** the leaves

D. **fertilize / feed** the plants

E. **plant** a tree

F. **water** the plants

G. **weed** the flower beds

H. **install** a sprinkler system

Use the new words.
Look at page 53. Name what you can do in the yard.

A: I can <u>mow the lawn</u>.
B: I can <u>weed the flower bed</u>.

Ask your classmates. Share the answers.
1. Do you know someone who does landscaping? Who?
2. Do you enjoy gardening? Why or why not?
3. Which gardening activity is the hardest to do? Why?

Crops

1. rice
2. wheat
3. soybeans
4. corn
5. alfalfa
6. cotton

7. field	12. farm equipment	17. corral	22. rancher
8. farmworker	13. farmer / grower	18. hay	A. **plant**
9. tractor	14. vegetable garden	19. fence	B. **harvest**
10. orchard	15. livestock	20. hired hand	C. **milk**
11. barn	16. vineyard	21. cattle	D. **feed**

1. construction worker
2. ladder
3. I beam/girder

4. scaffolding
5. cherry picker
6. bulldozer

7. crane
8. backhoe
9. jackhammer / pneumatic drill

10. concrete
11. tile
12. bricks

13. trowel
14. insulation
15. stucco

16. window pane
17. wood / lumber
18. plywood

19. drywall
20. shingles
21. pickax

22. shovel
23. sledgehammer

A. **paint**

B. **lay** bricks

C. **install** tile

D. **hammer**

Safety Hazards and Hazardous Materials

1. careless worker
2. careful worker

3. poisonous fumes
4. broken equipment

5. frayed cord
6. slippery floor

7. radioactive materials
8. flammable liquids

Safety Equipment

9. hard hat
10. safety glasses
11. safety goggles
12. safety visor

13. respirator
14. particle mask
15. ear plugs
16. earmuffs

17. work gloves
18. back support belt
19. knee pads
20. safety boots

21. fire extinguisher
22. two-way radio

HAND TOOLS

HARDWARE

POWER TOOLS

1. hammer	**4.** handsaw	**7.** pliers	**10.** jigsaw
2. mallet	**5.** hacksaw	**8.** electric drill	**11.** power sander
3. ax	**6.** C-clamp	**9.** circular saw	**12.** router

26. vise	**30.** screwdriver	**34.** nail	**38.** toggle bolt
27. blade	**31.** Phillips screwdriver	**35.** bolt	**39.** hook
28. drill bit	**32.** machine screw	**36.** nut	**40.** eye hook
29. level	**33.** wood screw	**37.** washer	**41.** chain

Use the new words.
Look at pages 62–63. Name the tools you see.

A: *There's a hammer.*
B: *There's a pipe wrench.*

Ask your classmates. Share the answers.
1. Are you good with tools?
2. Which tools do you have at home?
3. Where can you shop for building supplies?

ELECTRICAL

PLUMBING

LUMBER

PAINT

13. wire

14. extension cord

15. bungee cord

16. yardstick

17. pipe

18. fittings

19. 2 x 4 (two by four)

20. particle board

21. spray gun

22. paintbrush

23. paint roller

24. wood stain

25. paint

42. wire stripper

43. electrical tape

44. work light

45. tape measure

46. outlet cover

47. pipe wrench

48. adjustable wrench

49. duct tape

50. plunger

51. paint pan

52. scraper

53. masking tape

54. drop cloth

55. chisel

56. sandpaper

57. plane

Role play. Find an item in a building supply store.

A: *Where can I find particle board?*
B: *It's on the back wall, in the lumber section.*
A: *Great. And where are the nails?*

Think about it. Discuss.

1. Which tools are the most important to have? Why?
2. Which tools can be dangerous? Why?
3. Do you borrow tools from friends? Why or why not?

181

1. supply cabinet
2. clerk
3. janitor
4. conference room
5. executive
6. presentation
7. cubicle
8. office manager
9. desk
10. file clerk
11. file cabinet
12. computer technician
13. PBX
14. receptionist
15. reception area
16. waiting area

Ways to greet a receptionist

I'm here for a <u>job interview</u>.
I have a <u>9:00 a.m.</u> appointment with <u>Mr. Lee</u>.
I'd like to leave a message <u>for Mr. Lee</u>.

Role play. Talk to a receptionist.

A: *Hello. How can I help you?*
B: <u>*I'm here for a job interview with Mr. Lee.*</u>
A: *OK. What is your name?*

Office Equipment

17. computer
18. inkjet printer
19. laser printer

20. scanner
21. fax machine
22. paper cutter

23. photocopier
24. paper shredder
25. calculator

26. electric pencil sharpener
27. postal scale

Office Supplies

28. stapler
29. staples
30. clear tape
31. paper clip
32. packing tape
33. glue

34. rubber band
35. pushpin
36. correction fluid
37. correction tape
38. legal pad
39. sticky notes

40. mailer
41. mailing label
42. letterhead / stationery
43. envelope
44. rotary card file
45. ink cartridge

46. ink pad
47. stamp
48. appointment book
49. organizer
50. file folder

1. doorman	4. concierge	7. bellhop	10. guest
2. revolving door	5. gift shop	8. luggage cart	11. desk clerk
3. parking attendant	6. bell captain	9. elevator	12. front desk

13. guest room	15. king-size bed	17. room service	19. housekeeping cart
14. double bed	16. suite	18. hallway	20. housekeeper

21. pool service	23. maintenance	25. meeting room
22. pool	24. gym	26. ballroom

A Restaurant Kitchen

1. short-order cook	**3.** walk-in freezer	**5.** storeroom	**7.** head chef / executive chef
2. dishwasher	**4.** food preparation worker	**6.** sous chef	

Restaurant Dining

8. server	**11.** maitre d'	**14.** banquet room
9. diner	**12.** headwaiter	**15.** runner
10. buffet	**13.** bus person	**16.** caterer

More vocabulary

line cook: short-order cook
wait staff: servers, headwaiters, and runners

Ask your classmates. Share the answers.

1. Have you ever worked in a hotel? What did you do?
2. What is the hardest job in a hotel?
3. Would you prefer to stay at a hotel in the city or in the country?

1. dangerous
2. clinic
3. budget
4. floor plan
5. contractor
6. electrical hazard
7. wiring
8. bricklayer
A. **call in** sick

HEALTH CENTER

HARD HAT AREA

**Look at the picture.
What do you see?**

Answer the questions.

1. How many workers are there? How many are working?

2. Why did two workers call in sick?

3. What is dangerous at the construction site?

📖 Read the story.

A Bad Day at Work

Sam Lopez is the <u>contractor</u> for a new building. He makes the schedule and supervises the <u>budget</u>. He also solves problems. Today there are a lot of problems.

Two <u>bricklayers</u> <u>called in sick</u> this morning. Now Sam has only one bricklayer at work. One hour later, a construction worker fell. Now he has to go to the <u>clinic</u>. Sam always tells his workers to be careful. Construction work is <u>dangerous</u>. Sam's also worried because the new <u>wiring</u> is an <u>electrical hazard</u>.

Right now, the building owner is in Sam's office. Her new <u>floor plan</u> has 25 more offices. Sam has a headache. Maybe he needs to call in sick tomorrow.

Think about it.

1. What do you say when you can't come in to work? to school?

2. Imagine you are Sam. What do you tell the building owner? Why?

1. preschool / nursery school

2. elementary school

3. middle school / junior high school

4. high school

5. vocational school / technical school

6. community college

7. college / university

8. adult school

Listen and point. Take turns.

A: *Point to the preschool.*
B: *Point to the high school.*
A: *Point to the adult school.*

Dictate to your partner. Take turns.

A: *Write preschool.*
B: *Is that p-r-e-s-c-h-o-o-l?*
A: *Yes. That's right.*

9. language arts

10. math

11. science

12. history

13. world languages

14. ESL / ESOL

15. arts

16. music

17. physical education

More vocabulary

core course: a subject students have to take. Math is a core course.

elective: a subject students choose to take. Art is an elective.

Pair practice. Make new conversations.

A: *I go to* <u>community college</u>.

B: *What subjects are you taking?*

A: *I'm taking* <u>history</u> *and* <u>science</u>.

English Composition

1 factory

1. word

2 I worked in a factory.

2. sentence

3 Little by little, work and success came to me. My first job wasn't good. I worked in a small factory. Now, I help manage two factories.

3. paragraph

4

4. essay

Parts of an Essay

5. title

6. introduction

7. body

8. conclusion

9. quotation

10. footnote

Carlos Lopez
Eng. Comp.
10/21/10

5 Success in the U.S.

6 I came to Los Angeles from Mexico in 2006. I had no job, no friends, and no family here. I was homesick and scared, but I did not go home. I took English classes (always at night) and I studied hard. I believed in my future success!

7 More than 400,000 new immigrants come to the U.S every year. Most of us need to find work. During my first year here, my routine was the same: get up; look for work; go to class; go to bed. I had to take jobs with long hours and low pay. Often I had two or three jobs.

Little by little, work and success came to me. My first job wasn't good. I worked in a small factory. Now, I help manage two factories.

8 Hard work makes success possible. Henry David Thoreau said, "Men are born to succeed, not fail." My story shows that he was right. **9**

10 ¹ U.S. Census

Punctuation

. **11.** period

? **12.** question mark

! **13.** exclamation mark

, **14.** comma

" " **15.** quotation marks

' **16.** apostrophe

: **17.** colon

; **18.** semicolon

( ) **19.** parentheses

- **20.** hyphen

Writing Rules

A

Carlos

Mexico

Los Angeles

A. **Capitalize** names.

B

Hard work makes success possible.

B. **Capitalize** the first letter in a sentence.

C

I was homesick and scared, but I did not go home.

C. **Use** punctuation.

D

　I came to Los Angeles from Mexico in 2006. I had no job, no friends, and no family here. I was homesick and scared, but I did not go home. I took English classes (always at night) and I studied hard. I believed in my future success!

D. **Indent** the first sentence in a paragraph.

Ways to ask for suggestions on your compositions

What do you think of this title?
Is this paragraph OK? Is the punctuation correct?
Do you have any suggestions for the conclusion?

Pair practice. Make new conversations.

A: *What do you think of this title?*
B: *I think you need to revise it.*
A: *Thanks. Do you have any more suggestions?*

The Writing Process

PREWRITING

E. **Think about** the assignment.

F. **Brainstorm** ideas.

G. **Organize** your ideas.

WRITING AND REVISING

H. **Write** a first draft.

I. **Edit**. / **Proofread**.

J. **Revise**. / **Rewrite**.

SHARING AND RESPONDING

K. **Get** feedback.

L. **Write** a final draft.

M. **Turn in** your paper.

Ask your classmates. Share the answers.

1. Do you like to write essays?
2. Which part of the writing process do you like best? least?

Think about it. Discuss.

1. In which jobs are writing skills important?
2. What tools can help you edit your writing?
3. What are some good subjects for essays?

191

Mathematics

Integers

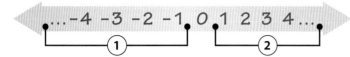

1. negative integers

2. positive integers

Fractions

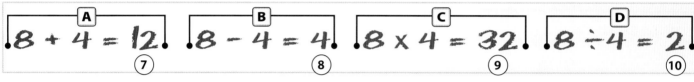

3. odd numbers

4. even numbers

5. numerator

6. denominator

Math Operations

A. add **B. subtract** **C. multiply** **D. divide**

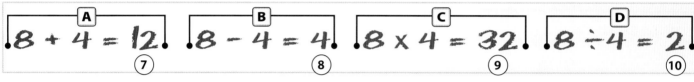

7. sum

8. difference

9. product

10. quotient

A Math Problem

11. Tom is 10 years older than Kim. Next year he will be twice as old as Kim. How old is Tom this year?

12. x = Kim's age now
$x + 10$ = Tom's age now
$x + 1$ = Kim's age next year
$2(x + 1)$ = Tom's age next year

13. $x + 10 + 1 = 2(x + 1)$
$x + 11 = 2x + 2$
$11 - 2 = 2x - x$

14. **$x = 9$, Kim is 9, Tom is 19**

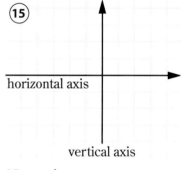

15. horizontal axis / vertical axis

11. word problem   12. variable   13. equation   14. solution   15. graph

Types of Math

How much are they?

$79 NOW 40% OFF!

x = the sale price
x = 79.00 - .40 (79.00)
x = $47.40

16. algebra

How many do I need?

area of path = 24 square ft.
area of brick = 2 square ft.
24 / 2 = 12 bricks

17. geometry

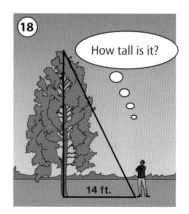

How tall is it?

14 ft.

tan 63° = height / 14 feet
height = 14 feet (tan 63°)
height ≈ 27.48 feet

18. trigonometry

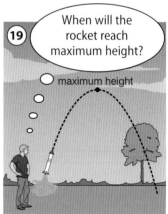

When will the rocket reach maximum height?

maximum height

$s(t) = -\frac{1}{2} g t^2 + V_0 t + h$
$s^{|}(t) = -gt + V_0 = 0$
$t = V_0 / g$

19. calculus

192

Mathematics

Lines

Angles

Shapes

20. line segment
21. endpoint
22. straight line
23. curved line
24. perpendicular lines

25. parallel lines
26. right angle / 90° angle
27. obtuse angle
28. acute angle

29. rectangle
30. square
31. diagonal
32. triangle
33. parallelogram

34. circle
35. radius
36. circumference
37. diameter

Geometric Solids

38. cube
39. pyramid
40. cone

41. cylinder
42. sphere

Measuring Area and Volume

  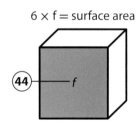

$\ell \times w = \text{area}$

$6 \times f = \text{surface area}$

$\pi \times r^2 \times h = \text{volume}$

$\frac{4}{3} \times \pi \times r^3 = \text{volume}$

$\pi \approx 3.14$

43. perimeter
44. face
45. base
46. pi

Ask your classmates. Share the answers.
1. Are you good at math?
2. Which types of math are easy for you?
3. Which types of math are difficult for you?

Think about it. Discuss.
1. What's the best way to learn mathematics?
2. How can you find the area of your classroom?
3. Which jobs use math? Which don't?

193

Biology

1. organisms
2. biologist
3. slide
4. cell
5. cell wall
6. cell membrane
7. nucleus
8. chromosome
9. cytoplasm

10. photosynthesis

THE DESERT

THE OCEAN

11. habitat
12. vertebrates
13. invertebrates

A Microscope

14. eyepiece
15. revolving nosepiece
16. objective
17. stage
18. diaphragm
19. light source
20. base
21. stage clips
22. fine adjustment knob
23. arm
24. coarse adjustment knob

Chemistry

25. chemist
26. periodic table
27. molecule

28. atom
29. nucleus
30. electron

31. proton
32. neutron
33. physicist

Physics

34. formula
35. prism
36. magnet

A Science Lab

37. Bunsen burner
38. graduated cylinder
39. beaker

40. funnel
41. balance / scale
42. test tube

43. forceps
44. crucible tongs
45. dropper

An Experiment

A. **State** a hypothesis.

B. **Do** an experiment.

C. **Observe.**

D. **Record** the results.

E. **Draw** a conclusion.

Desktop Computer

1. surge protector	6. hard drive	11. monitor /screen	16. laptop
2. power cord	7. USB port	12. webcam	17. printer
3. tower	8. flash drive	13. cable	
4. microprocessor / CPU	9. DVD and CD-ROM drive	14. keyboard	
5. motherboard	10. software	15. mouse	

Keyboarding

A. **type**   B. **select**   C. **delete**   D. **go to** the next line

Navigating a Webpage

1. menu bar	**4.** URL / website address	**7.** tab	**10.** links	**13.** text box
2. back button	**5.** search box	**8.** drop-down menu	**11.** video player	**14.** cursor
3. forward button	**6.** search engine	**9.** pop-up ad	**12.** pointer	**15.** scroll bar

Logging on and Sending Email

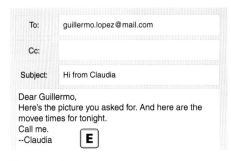

A. type your password

C. address the email

E. type the message

B. click "sign in"

D. type the subject

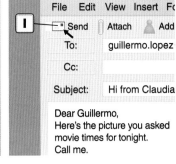

F. check your spelling

G. attach a picture

H. attach a file

I. send the email

Colonial Period

New Hampshire
Massachusetts
Connecticut
New York
Rhode Island
Pennsylvania
New Jersey
Delaware
Virginia
Maryland
North Carolina
South Carolina
Georgia

1. thirteen colonies
2. colonists
3. Native Americans
4. slave
5. Declaration of Independence
6. First Continental Congress
7. founders
8. Revolutionary War
9. redcoat
10. minuteman
11. first president
12. Constitution
13. Bill of Rights

Western Expansion 1803 – 1893

Civil War 1861 – 1865

World War I 1914 – 1918

Jazz Age 1920 – 1929

World War II 1941 – 1945

Civil Rights Movement 1954 – 1972

Information Age 1959 – now

1800   1850   1900   1950   2000 →

Industrial Revolution 1793 – 1908

14th Amendment Citizenship for African American males
15th Amendment Voting rights for African American males
1st African American senator: H. Revels
Reconstruction 1865 – 1877

WORKERS UNITE!
Progressivism 1889 – 1916

COFFEE & DOUGHNUTS FOR THE UNEMPLOYED
Great Depression 1929 – 1941

NUCLEAR WAR
Cold War 1945 – 1989

Space Age 1958 – now

Global Age 1994 – now

Civilizations

Pyramids
Parthenon
1

Times Square
2

Caesar

Qin Shi Huang

3

King Henry VIII

Queen Elizabeth I

4

5
Juarez

Mussolini
6

Churchill
7

1. ancient

2. modern

3. emperor

4. monarch

5. president

6. dictator

7. prime minister

Historical Terms

Vikings
Astronauts
8
9

10
11

12
13

8. exploration

9. explorer

10. war

11. army

12. immigration

13. immigrant

Mozart
Duke Ellington
14
15

Susan B. Anthony
César Chávez
16
17

Edison
Camarena
18
19

14. composer

15. composition

16. political movement

17. activist

18. inventor

19. invention

Lesser Antilles

Puerto Rico (US)

DOMINICAN REPUBLIC

HAITI

Hispaniola

CUBA

Greater Antilles

JAMAICA

Caribbean Sea

NICARAGUA

PANAMA

BELIZE

HONDURAS

COSTA RICA

EL SALVADOR

GUATEMALA

(19)

Yucatán

Quintana Roo

Campeche

Tabasco

Chiapas

Veracruz

Tlaxcala

Puebla

Oaxaca

(18)

Morelos

Guerrero

(17)

DISTRITO FEDERAL

Michoacán

Colima

Jalisco

Nayarit

Guanajuato

Aguascalientes

Zacatecas

San Luis Potosí

Tamaulipas

Querétaro

Hidalgo

México

(16)

EAST

NORTH

SOUTH

WEST

Regions of Canada

1. Northern Canada

2. British Columbia

3. The Prairie Provinces

4. Ontario

5. Québec

6. The Maritime Provinces

Regions of the United States

7. The Pacific States / the West Coast

8. The Rocky Mountain States

9. The Midwest

10. The Mid-Atlantic States

11. New England

12. The Southwest

13. The Southeast / the South

Regions of Mexico

14. The Pacific Northwest

15. The Plateau of Mexico

16. The Gulf Coastal Plain

17. The Southern Uplands

18. The Chiapas Highlands

19. The Yucatan Peninsula

Continents

1. North America

2. South America

3. Europe

4. Asia

5. Africa

6. Australia

7. Antarctica

1. rain forest	**6.** ocean	**10.** beach	**14.** mountain peak	**18.** valley
2. waterfall	**7.** peninsula	**11.** forest	**15.** mountain range	**19.** plains
3. river	**8.** island	**12.** shore	**16.** hills	**20.** meadow
4. desert	**9.** bay	**13.** lake	**17.** canyon	**21.** pond
5. sand dune				

More vocabulary

a body of water: a river, lake, or ocean
stream / creek: a very small river

Ask your classmates. Share the answers.

1. Would you rather live near a river or a lake?
2. Would you rather travel through a forest or a desert?
3. How often do you go to the beach or the shore?

The Solar System and the Planets

Sun
1
2
3
4
5
6
7
8
Asteroid Belt
Orbit

1. Mercury	**3.** Earth	**5.** Jupiter	**7.** Uranus
2. Venus	**4.** Mars	**6.** Saturn	**8.** Neptune

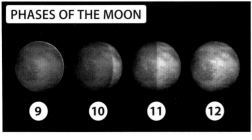

PHASES OF THE MOON
9 10 11 12

SPACE
13 14 15

16

9. new moon	**11.** quarter moon	**13.** star	**15.** galaxy
10. crescent moon	**12.** full moon	**14.** constellation	**16.** solar eclipse

SPACE EXPLORATION
17 18 19 20

ASTRONOMY
21 22 23 24

17. astronaut	**19.** space shuttle	**21.** observatory	**23.** telescope
18. space station	**20.** satellite	**22.** astronomer	**24.** comet

---

More vocabulary

solar eclipse: when the moon is between the earth and the sun
Big Dipper: a famous part of the constellation Ursa Major
Sirius: the brightest star in the night sky

Ask your classmates. Share the answers.

1. How do you feel when you look at the night sky?
2. Can you name one or more constellations?
3. Do you want to travel in space?

A Graduation

Home | Search | Invite | Mail |

All Adelia's photos

I loved Art History.

My last economics lesson

Marching Band is great!

The photographer was upset.

We look good!

I get my diploma.

Dad and his digital camera

1. photographer
2. funny photo
3. serious photo
4. guest speaker
5. podium
6. ceremony
7. cap
8. gown

A. **take** a picture
B. **cry**
C. **celebrate**

People	Comments	
Sara	**June 29th 8:19 p.m.**	
	Great pictures! What a day!	Delete
Zannie baby	**June 30th 10 a.m.**	
	Love the funny photo.	Delete

I'm behind the mayor.

We're all very happy.

Look at the pictures. What do you see?

Answer the questions.

1. How many people are wearing caps and gowns?

2. How many people are being funny? How many are being serious?

3. Who is standing at the podium?

4. Why are the graduates throwing their caps in the air?

 Read the story.

A Graduation

Look at these great photos on my web page! The first three are from my favorite classes, but the other pictures are from graduation day.

There are two pictures of my classmates in <u>caps</u> and <u>gowns</u>. In the first picture, we're laughing and the <u>photographer</u> is upset. In the second photo, we're serious. I like the <u>serious photo</u>, but I love the <u>funny photo</u>!

There's also a picture of our <u>guest speaker</u>, the mayor. She is standing at the <u>podium</u>. Next, you can see me at the graduation <u>ceremony</u>. My dad wanted to <u>take a picture</u> of me with my diploma. That's my mom next to him. She <u>cries</u> when she's happy.

After the ceremony, everyone was happy, but no one cried. We wanted to <u>celebrate</u> and we did!

Think about it.

1. What kinds of ceremonies are important for children? for teens? for adults?

2. Imagine you are the guest speaker at a graduation. What will you say to the graduates?

207

Nature Center

1. trees

2. soil

3. path

4. bird

5. plants

6. rock

7. flowers

Listen and point. Take turns.

A: *Point to the trees.*
B: *Point to a bird.*
A: *Point to the flowers.*

Dictate to your partner. Take turns.

A: *Write it's a tree.*
B: *Let me check that. I-t-'s -a- t-r-e-e?*
A: *Yes, that's right.*

8.	sun
9.	sky
10.	mammals
11.	insects
12.	nest
13.	water
14.	fish

Ways to talk about nature

Look at the sky! Isn't it beautiful?
Did you see the fish / insects?
It's / They're so interesting.

Pair practice. Make new conversations.

A: *Do you know the name of that yellow flower?*
B: *I think it's a sunflower.*
A: *Oh, and what about that blue bird?*

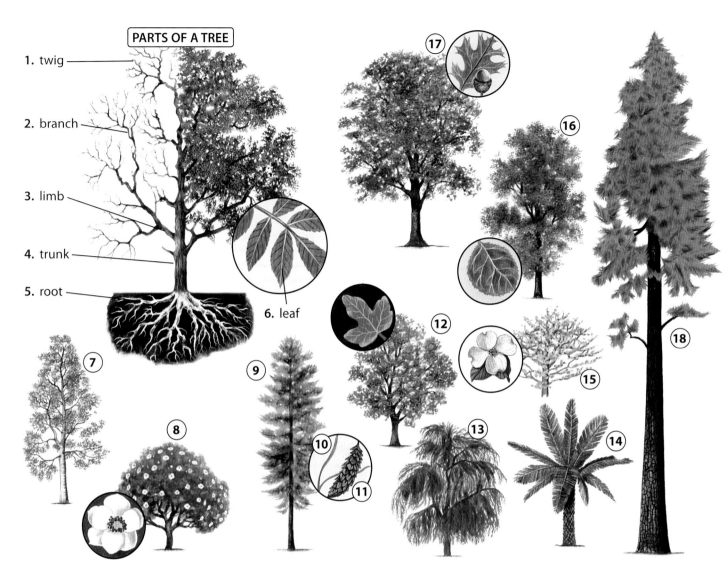

PARTS OF A TREE

1. twig
2. branch
3. limb
4. trunk
5. root
6. leaf

7. birch	10. needle	13. willow	16. elm
8. magnolia	11. pinecone	14. palm	17. oak
9. pine	12. maple	15. dogwood	18. redwood

Plants

19. holly	21. cactus	23. poison sumac	25. poison ivy
20. berries	22. vine	24. poison oak	

Parts of a Flower

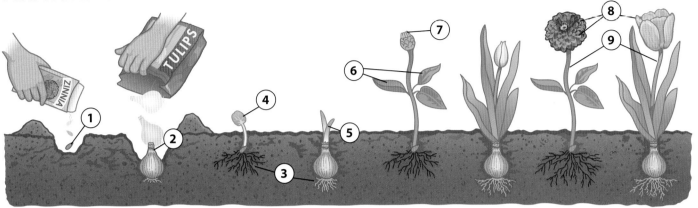

1. seed	**4.** seedling	**7.** bud
2. bulb	**5.** shoot	**8.** petals
3. roots	**6.** leaves	**9.** stems

10. sunflower	**15.** rose	**20.** carnation	**25.** daffodil
11. tulip	**16.** iris	**21.** chrysanthemum	**26.** lily
12. hibiscus	**17.** crocus	**22.** jasmine	**27.** houseplant
13. marigold	**18.** gardenia	**23.** violet	**28.** bouquet
14. daisy	**19.** orchid	**24.** poinsettia	**29.** thorn

Sea Animals

PARTS OF A FISH

1. fin
2. gills
3. scales

4. shark	**9.** octopus	**14.** jellyfish	**19.** scallop	**24.** sea anemone
5. cod	**10.** swordfish	**15.** flounder	**20.** crab	
6. bass	**11.** ray	**16.** starfish	**21.** sea urchin	
7. squid	**12.** eel	**17.** mussel	**22.** snail	
8. tuna	**13.** seahorse	**18.** shrimp	**23.** worm	

Amphibians

25. frog   **26.** newt   **27.** salamander   **28.** toad

Sea Mammals

29. whale	**31.** dolphin	**33.** sea lion	**35.** sea otter
30. porpoise	**32.** walrus	**34.** seal	

Reptiles

36. alligator	**38.** rattlesnake	**40.** lizard	**42.** tortoise
37. crocodile	**39.** garter snake	**41.** cobra	**43.** turtle

PARTS OF A BIRD

1. wing
2. claw
3. beak / bill
4. feather

5. owl	8. woodpecker	11. penguin	14. peacock
6. blue jay	9. eagle	12. duck	15. pigeon
7. sparrow	10. hummingbird	13. goose	16. robin

Insects and Arachnids

17. wasp	21. moth	25. honeybee	29. spider
18. beetle	22. mosquito	26. ladybug	30. scorpion
19. butterfly	23. cricket	27. tick	
20. caterpillar	24. grasshopper	28. fly	

214

Farm Animals

1. cow	**3.** donkey	**5.** goat	**7.** rooster
2. pig	**4.** horse	**6.** sheep	**8.** hen

Pets

9. cat	**11.** dog	**13.** rabbit	**15.** parakeet
10. kitten	**12.** puppy	**14.** guinea pig	**16.** goldfish

Rodents

17. rat	**19.** gopher	**21.** squirrel
18. mouse	**20.** chipmunk	**22.** prairie dog

More vocabulary

domesticated: animals that work for and / or live with people

wild: animals that live away from people

Ask your classmates. Share the answers.

1. Have you worked with farm animals? Which ones?
2. Are you afraid of rodents? Which ones?
3. Do you have a pet? What kind?

215

1. moose
2. mountain lion
3. coyote
4. opossum

5. wolf
6. buffalo / bison
7. bat
8. armadillo

9. beaver
10. porcupine
11. bear
12. skunk

13. raccoon
14. deer
15. fox

16. antlers
17. hooves

18. whiskers
19. coat / fur

20. paw
21. horn

22. tail
23. quill

24. anteater	**29.** gorilla	**34.** leopard	**39.** orangutan	**44.** kangaroo
25. llama	**30.** hyena	**35.** antelope	**40.** panther	**45.** koala
26. monkey	**31.** baboon	**36.** lion	**41.** panda	**46.** platypus
27. chimpanzee	**32.** giraffe	**37.** tiger	**42.** elephant	
28. rhinoceros	**33.** zebra	**38.** camel	**43.** hippopotamus	

47. trunk   **48.** tusk   **49.** mane   **50.** pouch   **51.** hump

Energy Sources

1. solar energy

2. wind power

3. natural gas

4. coal

5. hydroelectric power

6. oil / petroleum

7. geothermal energy

8. nuclear energy

9. biomass / bioenergy

10. fusion

Pollution

11. air pollution / smog

12. hazardous waste

13. acid rain

14. water pollution

15. radiation

16. pesticide poisoning

17. oil spill

Ask your classmates. Share the answers.
1. What types of things do you recycle?
2. What types of energy sources are in your area?
3. What types of pollution do you worry about?

Think about it. Discuss.
1. How can you save energy in the summer? winter?
2. What are some other ways that people can conserve energy or prevent pollution?

Ways to Conserve Energy and Resources

A. **reduce** trash

B. **reuse** shopping bags

C. **recycle**

D. **buy** recycled products

E. **save** water

F. **fix** leaky faucets

G. **turn off** lights

H. **use** energy-efficient bulbs

I. **carpool**

J. **adjust** the thermostat

K. **wash** clothes in cold water

L. **don't litter**

M. **compost** food scraps

N. **plant** a tree

Yosemite
NATIONAL PARK

Half Dome

1

2

3

Dry Tortugas
NATIONAL PARK

Fort Jefferson

4

5

1. landmarks	3. wildlife	5. coral	7. caverns
2. park ranger	4. ferry	6. cave	A. **take** a tour

CARLSBAD
CAVERNS
NATIONAL PARK

6

7

A

**Look at the pictures.
What do you see?**

Answer the questions.

1. How many U.S. landmarks are in the pictures?

2. What kinds of wildlife do you see?

3. What can you do at Carlsbad Caverns?

📖 **Read the story.**

U.S. National Parks

More than 200 million people visit U.S. National Parks every year. These parks protect the wildlife and landmarks of the United States. Each park is different, and each one is beautiful.

At Yosemite, in California, you can take a nature walk with a park ranger. You'll see waterfalls, redwoods, and deer there.

In south Florida, you can take a ferry to Dry Tortugas. It's great to snorkel around the park's coral islands.

There are 113 caves at Carlsbad Caverns in New Mexico. The deepest cave is 830 feet below the desert! You can take a tour of these beautiful caverns.

There are 391 national parks to see. Go online for information about a park near you.

Think about it.

1. Why are national parks important?

2. Imagine you are a park ranger at a national park. Give your classmates a tour of the landmarks and wildlife.

Places to Go

1. zoo

2. movies

3. botanical garden

4. bowling alley

5. rock concert

6. swap meet / flea market

7. aquarium

Places to Go in Our City

Listen and point. Take turns.

A: *Point to the zoo.*
B: *Point to the flea market.*
A: *Point to the rock concert.*

Dictate to your partner. Take turns.

A: *Write these words: zoo, movies, aquarium.*
B: *Zoo, movies, and what?*
A: *Aquarium.*

8. play

9. art museum

10. amusement park

11. opera

12. nightclub

13. county fair

14. classical concert

Ways to make plans using *Let's go*

Let's go to the amusement park tomorrow.

Let's go to the opera on Saturday.

Let's go to the movies tonight.

Pair practice. Make new conversations.

A: *Let's go to the zoo this afternoon.*

B: *OK. And let's go to the movies tonight.*

A: *That sounds like a good plan.*

223

1. ball field	5. fountain	9. water fountain	13. slide
2. cyclist	6. tennis court	10. bench	14. climbing apparatus
3. bike path	7. skateboard	11. swings	15. sandbox
4. jump rope	8. picnic table	12. tricycle	16. seesaw

A. pull the wagon

B. push the swing

C. climb the bars

D. picnic / have a picnic

1. ocean / water	7. fins	13. shade	19. lifeguard
2. kite	8. pail / bucket	14. beach umbrella	20. lifesaving device
3. sailboat	9. cooler	15. surfer	21. lifeguard station
4. wet suit	10. sunscreen / sunblock	16. surfboard	22. beach chair
5. scuba tank	11. blanket	17. wave	23. sand
6. diving mask	12. sand castle	18. pier	24. seashell

More vocabulary

seaweed: a plant that grows in the ocean
tide: the level of the ocean. The tide goes in and out every 12 hours.

Ask your classmates. Share the answers.

1. Do you like to go to the beach?
2. Are there famous beaches in your native country?
3. Do you prefer to be on the sand or in the water?

225

1. boating
2. rafting
3. canoeing

4. fishing
5. camping
6. backpacking

7. hiking
8. mountain biking
9. horseback riding

10. tent
11. campfire
12. sleeping bag
13. foam pad
14. life vest

15. backpack
16. camping stove
17. fishing net
18. fishing pole
19. rope

20. multi-use knife
21. matches
22. lantern
23. insect repellent
24. canteen

1. downhill skiing

2. snowboarding

3. cross-country skiing

4. ice skating

5. figure skating

6. sledding

7. waterskiing

8. sailing

9. surfing

10. windsurfing

11. snorkeling

12. scuba diving

More vocabulary

speed skating: racing while ice skating
windsurfing: sailboarding

Ask your classmates. Share the answers.

1. Which of these sports do you like?
2. Which of these sports would you like to learn?
3. Which of these sports is the most fun to watch?

227

1. archery

2. billiards / pool

3. bowling

4. boxing

5. cycling / biking

6. badminton

7. fencing

8. golf

9. gymnastics

10. inline skating

11. martial arts

12. racquetball

13. skateboarding

14. table tennis

15. tennis

16. weightlifting

17. wrestling

18. track and field

19. horse racing

Pair practice. Make new conversations.

A: *What sports do you like?*
B: *I like <u>bowling</u>. What do you like?*
A: *I like <u>gymnastics</u>.*

Think about it. Discuss.

1. Why do people like to watch sports?
2. Which sports can be dangerous?
3. Why do people do dangerous sports?

1. score	**3.** team	**5.** player	**7.** basketball court
2. coach	**4.** fan	**6.** official / referee	

8. basketball

9. baseball

10. softball

11. football

12. soccer

13. ice hockey

14. volleyball

15. water polo

More Vocabulary

win: to have the best score
lose: the opposite of win
tie: to have the same score

captain: the team leader
umpire: the name of the referee in baseball
Little League: a baseball and softball program for children

A. pitch

B. hit

C. throw

D. catch

E. kick

F. tackle

G. pass

H. shoot

I. jump

J. dribble

K. dive

L. swim

M. stretch

N. exercise / work out

O. bend

P. serve

Q. swing

R. start

S. race

T. finish

U. skate

V. ski

Use the new words.
Look on page 229. Name the actions you see.

A: He's _throwing_.

B: She's _jumping_.

Ways to talk about your sports skills

I can _throw_, but I can't _catch_.

I _swim_ well, but I don't _dive_ well.

I'm good at _skating_, but I'm terrible at _skiing_.

230

1. golf club	**8.** arrow	**15.** catcher's mask	**22.** weights
2. tennis racket	**9.** ice skates	**16.** uniform	**23.** snowboard
3. volleyball	**10.** inline skates	**17.** glove	**24.** skis
4. basketball	**11.** hockey stick	**18.** baseball	**25.** ski poles
5. bowling ball	**12.** soccer ball	**19.** football helmet	**26.** ski boots
6. bow	**13.** shin guards	**20.** shoulder pads	**27.** flying disc*
7. target	**14.** baseball bat	**21.** football	*__Note:__ one brand is Frisbee®, of Wham-O, Inc.

Use the new words.

Look at pages 228–229. Name the sports equipment you see.

A: *Those are ice skates.*

B: *That's a football.*

Ask your classmates. Share the answers.

1. Do you own any sports equipment? What kind?
2. What do you want to buy at this store?
3. Where is the best place to buy sports equipment?

231

A. **collect** things   B. **play** games   C. **quilt**   D. **do** crafts

1. figurine	5. board game	9. model kit	13. doll making kit
2. baseball cards	6. dice	10. acrylic paint	14. woodworking kit
3. video game console	7. checkers	11. glue stick	15. quilt block
4. video game control	8. chess	12. construction paper	16. rotary cutter

Grammar Point: *How often do you play cards?*

*I play **all the time**. (every day)*

*I play **sometimes**. (once a month)*

*I **never** play. (0 times)*

Pair practice. Make new conversations.

A: *How often do you do your hobbies?*

B: *I <u>play games</u> all the time. I love <u>chess</u>.*

A: *Really? I never play <u>chess</u>.*

E. paint   **F. knit**   **G. pretend**   **H. play** cards

17. canvas

18. easel

19. oil paint

20. paintbrush

21. watercolor

22. yarn

23. knitting needles

24. embroidery

25. crocheting

26. action figure

27. model trains

28. paper dolls

29. diamonds

30. spades

31. hearts

32. clubs

Ways to talk about hobbies and games

*This <u>board game</u> is **interesting**. It makes me think.*
*That <u>video game</u> is **boring**. Nothing happens.*
*I love to <u>play cards</u>. It's **fun** to play with my friends.*

Ask your classmates. Share the answers.

1. Do you collect anything? What?
2. Which games do you like to play?
3. What hobbies did you have as a child?

233

1. CD boombox

2. MP3 player

3. dock

4. headphones

5. personal CD player

6. portable cassette player

7. flat screen TV / flat panel TV

8. portable TV

9. universal remote

10. DVD player

11. portable DVD player

12. turntable

13. tuner

14. speakers

15. adapter

16. plug

17. charger

18. microphone

19. digital camera	**23.** zoom lens	**27.** battery charger
20. memory card	**24.** camcorder	**28.** camera case
21. film camera / 35 mm camera	**25.** tripod	**29.** LCD projector
22. film	**26.** battery pack	**30.** screen

31. photo album	**33.** out of focus	**35.** underexposed
32. digital photo album	**34.** overexposed	

A. **record**	C. **rewind**	E. **pause**
B. **play**	D. **fast forward**	

Types of TV Programs

1. news program

2. sitcom (situation comedy)

3. cartoon

4. talk show

5. soap opera

6. reality show

7. nature program

8. game show

9. children's program

10. shopping program

11. sports program

12. drama

Types of Movies

13. comedy

14. tragedy

15. western

16. romance

17. horror story

18. science fiction story

19. action story / adventure story

20. mystery / suspense

Types of Music

21. classical

22. blues

23. rock

24. jazz

25. pop

26. hip hop

27. country

28. R&B / soul

29. folk

30. gospel

31. reggae

32. world music

A. play an instrument

B. sing a song

C. conduct an orchestra

D. be in a rock band

Woodwinds

1. flute
2. clarinet
3. oboe
4. bassoon
5. saxophone

Strings

6. violin
7. cello
8. bass
9. guitar

Brass

10. trombone
11. trumpet / horn
12. tuba
13. French horn

Percussion

14. piano
15. xylophone
16. drums
17. tambourine

Other Instruments

18. electric keyboard
19. accordion
20. organ
21. harmonica

1. parade	6. heart
2. float	7. fireworks
3. confetti	8. flag
4. couple	9. mask
5. card	10. jack-o'-lantern

11. costume	15. ornament
12. candy	16. Christmas tree
13. feast	17. candy cane
14. turkey	18. string lights

*Thanksgiving is on the fourth Thursday in November.

A Birthday Party

1. decorations
2. deck
3. present / gift

A. **videotape**
B. **make** a wish
C. **blow out**

D. **hide**
E. **bring**

F. **wrap**

240

Happy Birthday!

Look at the picture.
What do you see?

Answer the questions.

1. What kinds of decorations do you see?
2. What are people doing at this birthday party?
3. What wish did the teenager make?
4. How many presents did people bring?

Read the story.

A Birthday Party

Today is Lou and Gani Bombata's birthday barbecue. There are <u>decorations</u> around the backyard, and food and drinks on the <u>deck</u>. There are also <u>presents</u>. Everyone in the Bombata family likes to <u>bring</u> presents.

Right now, it's time for cake. Gani <u>is blowing out</u> the candles, and Lou <u>is making a wish</u>. Lou's mom wants to <u>videotape</u> everyone, but she can't find Lou's brother, Todd. Todd hates to sing, so he always <u>hides</u> for the birthday song.

Lou's sister, Amaka, has to <u>wrap</u> some <u>gifts</u>. She doesn't want Lou to see. Amaka isn't worried. She knows her family loves to sing. She can put her gifts on the present table before they finish the first song.

Think about it.

1. What wish do you think Gani made?
2. What kinds of presents do you give to relatives? What kinds of presents can you give to friends or co-workers?

241

Verb Guide

Verbs in English are either regular or irregular in the past tense and past participle forms.

Regular Verbs

The regular verbs below are marked 1, 2, 3, or 4 according to four different spelling patterns.
(See page 244 for the irregular verbs which do not follow any of these patterns.)

Spelling Patterns for the Past and the Past Participle	Example	
1. Add -ed to the end of the verb.	ASK	ASKED
2. Add -d to the end of the verb.	LIVE	LIVED
3. Double the final consonant and add -ed to the end of the verb.	DROP	DROPPED
4. Drop the final y and add -ied to the end of the verb.	CRY	CRIED

The Oxford Picture Dictionary List of Regular Verbs

accept (1)
add (1)
address (1)
adjust (1)
agree (2)
answer (1)
apologize (2)
appear (1)
applaud (1)
apply (4)
arrange (2)
arrest (1)
arrive (2)
ask (1)
assemble (2)
assist (1)
attach (1)
bake (2)
bank (1)
bargain (1)
bathe (2)
board (1)
boil (1)
borrow (1)
bow (1)
brainstorm (1)
breathe (2)
browse (2)
brush (1)
bubble (2)
buckle (2)
burn (1)
bus (1)
calculate (2)
call (1)
capitalize (2)
carpool (1)

carry (4)
cash (1)
celebrate (2)
change (2)
check (1)
chill (1)
choke (2)
chop (3)
circle (2)
claim (1)
clean (1)
clear (1)
click (1)
climb (1)
close (2)
collate (2)
collect (1)
color (1)
comb (1)
comfort (1)
commit (3)
compliment (1)
compost (1)
conceal (1)
conduct (1)
convert (1)
convict (1)
cook (1)
copy (4)
correct (1)
cough (1)
count (1)
cross (1)
cry (4)
dance (2)
debate (2)
decline (2)

delete (2)
deliver (1)
design (1)
dial (1)
dice (2)
dictate (2)
die (2)
disagree (2)
discipline (2)
discuss (1)
dive (2)
divide (2)
dress (1)
dribble (2)
drill (1)
drop (3)
drown (1)
dry (4)
dust (1)
dye (2)
edit (1)
empty (4)
enter (1)
erase (2)
evacuate (2)
examine (2)
exchange (2)
exercise (2)
expire (2)
explain (1)
exterminate (2)
fasten (1)
fast forward (1)
fax (1)
fertilize (2)
fill (1)
finish (1)

fix (1)
floss (1)
fold (1)
follow (1)
garden (1)
gargle (2)
graduate (2)
grate (2)
grease (2)
greet (1)
hail (1)
hammer (1)
hand (1)
harvest (1)
help (1)
hire (2)
hug (3)
immigrate (2)
indent (1)
inquire (2)
insert (1)
inspect (1)
install (1)
introduce (2)
invite (2)
iron (1)
jaywalk (1)
join (1)
jump (1)
kick (1)
kiss (1)
knit (3)
label (1)
land (1)
laugh (1)
learn (1)
lengthen (1)

lift (1)
listen (1)
litter (1)
live (2)
load (1)
lock (1)
look (1)
mail (1)
manufacture (2)
match (1)
measure (2)
microwave (2)
milk (1)
misbehave (2)
miss (1)
mix (1)
mop (3)
move (2)
mow (1)
multiply (4)
negotiate (2)
network (1)
numb (1)
nurse (2)
obey (1)
observe (2)
offer (1)
open (1)
operate (2)
order (1)
organize (2)
overdose (2)
pack (1)
paint (1)
park (1)
participate (2)
pass (1)
pause (2)
peel (1)
perm (1)
pick (1)

pitch (1)
plan (3)
plant (1)
play (1)
polish (1)
pour (1)
praise (2)
preheat (1)
prepare (2)
prescribe (2)
press (1)
pretend (1)
print (1)
program (3)
protect (1)
pull (1)
purchase (2)
push (1)
quilt (1)
race (2)
raise (2)
rake (2)
receive (2)
record (1)
recycle (2)
redecorate (2)
reduce (2)
register (1)
relax (1)
remain (1)
remove (2)
renew (1)
repair (1)
replace (2)
report (1)
request (1)
retire (2)
return (1)
reuse (2)
revise (2)
rinse (2)

rock (1)
sauté (1)
save (2)
scan (3)
schedule (2)
scrub (3)
seat (1)
select (1)
sentence (2)
separate (2)
serve (2)
share (2)
shave (2)
ship (3)
shop (3)
shorten (1)
sign (1)
simmer (1)
skate (2)
ski (1)
slice (2)
smell (1)
smile (2)
smoke (2)
sneeze (2)
solve (2)
sort (1)
spell (1)
spoon (1)
staple (2)
start (1)
state (2)
stay (1)
steam (1)
stir (3)
stop (3)
stow (1)
stretch (1)
study (4)
submit (3)
subtract (1)

supervise (2)
swallow (1)
tackle (2)
talk (1)
taste (2)
thank (1)
tie (2)
touch (1)
transcribe (2)
transfer (3)
translate (2)
travel (1)
trim (3)
try (4)
turn (1)
type (2)
underline (2)
undress (1)
unload (1)
unpack (1)
unscramble (2)
use (2)
vacuum (1)
videotape (2)
volunteer (1)
vomit (1)
vote (2)
wait (1)
walk (1)
wash (1)
watch (1)
water (1)
wave (2)
weed (1)
weigh (1)
wipe (2)
work (1)
wrap (3)

243

Irregular Verbs

These verbs have irregular endings in the past and/or the past participle.

The Oxford Picture Dictionary List of Irregular Verbs

simple	past	past participle	simple	past	past participle
be	was	been	make	made	made
beat	beat	beaten	meet	met	met
become	became	become	pay	paid	paid
bend	bent	bent	picnic	picnicked	picnicked
bleed	bled	bled	proofread	proofread	proofread
blow	blew	blown	put	put	put
break	broke	broken	read	read	read
bring	brought	brought	rewind	rewound	rewound
buy	bought	bought	rewrite	rewrote	rewritten
catch	caught	caught	ride	rode	ridden
choose	chose	chosen	run	ran	run
come	came	come	say	said	said
cut	cut	cut	see	saw	seen
do	did	done	seek	sought	sought
draw	drew	drawn	sell	sold	sold
drink	drank	drunk	send	sent	sent
drive	drove	driven	set	set	set
eat	ate	eaten	sew	sewed	sewn
fall	fell	fallen	shake	shook	shaken
feed	fed	fed	shoot	shot	shot
feel	felt	felt	show	showed	shown
find	found	found	sing	sang	sung
fly	flew	flown	sit	sat	sat
get	got	gotten	speak	spoke	spoken
give	gave	given	stand	stood	stood
go	went	gone	steal	stole	stolen
hang	hung	hung	sweep	swept	swept
have	had	had	swim	swam	swum
hear	heard	heard	swing	swung	swung
hide	hid	hidden	take	took	taken
hit	hit	hit	teach	taught	taught
hold	held	held	think	thought	thought
keep	kept	kept	throw	threw	thrown
lay	laid	laid	wake	woke	woken
leave	left	left	withdraw	withdrew	withdrawn
lend	lent	lent	write	wrote	written
let	let	let			

Index

Index Key

Font

bold type = verbs or verb phrases (example: **catch**)

ordinary type = all other parts of speech (example: baseball)

ALL CAPS = unit titles (example: MATHEMATICS)

Initial caps = subunit titles (example: Equivalencies)

Symbols

✦ = word found in exercise band at bottom of page

Numbers/Letters

first number in **bold** type = page on which word appears

second number, or letter, following number in **bold** type = item number on page

(examples: cool [ko͞ol] **13**-5 means that the word *cool* is item number 5 on page 13;

across [ə krös/] **153**–G means that the word *across* is item G on page 153).

Pronunciation Guide

The index includes a pronunciation guide for all the words and phrases illustrated in the book. This guide uses symbols commonly found in dictionaries for native speakers. These symbols, unlike those used in pronunciation systems such as the International Phonetic Alphabet, tend to use English spelling patterns and so should help you to become more aware of the connections between written English and spoken English.

Consonants

[b] as in back [băk]	[k] as in key [kē]	[sh] as in shoe [sho͞o]
[ch] as in cheek [chēk]	[l] as in leaf [lēf]	[t] as in tape [tāp]
[d] as in date [dāt]	[m] as in match [măch]	[th] as in three [thrē]
[dh] as in this [dhĭs]	[n] as in neck [nĕk]	[v] as in vine [vīn]
[f] as in face [fās]	[ng] as in ring [rĭng]	[w] as in wait [wāt]
[g] as in gas [găs]	[p] as in park [pärk]	[y] as in yams [yămz]
[h] as in half [hăf]	[r] as in rice [rīs]	[z] as in zoo [zo͞o]
[j] as in jam [jăm]	[s] as in sand [sănd]	[zh] as in measure [mĕzhər]

Vowels

[ā] as in bake [bāk]	[ī] as in line [līn]	[o͝o] as in cook [ko͝ok]
[ă] as in back [băk]	[ĭ] as in lip [lĭp]	[ow] as in cow [kow]
[ä] as in car [kär] or box [bäks]	[ï] as in near [nïr]	[oy] as in boy [boy]
[ē] as in beat [bēt]	[ō] as in cold [kōld]	[ŭ] as in cut [kŭt]
[ĕ] as in bed [bĕd]	[ö] as in short [shört] or claw [klö]	[ü] as in curb [kürb]
[ë] as in bear [bër]	[o͞o] as in cool [ko͞ol]	[ə] as in above [ə bŭv/]

All the pronunciation symbols used are alphabetical except for the schwa [ə]. The schwa is the most frequent vowel sound in English. If you use the schwa appropriately in unstressed syllables, your pronunciation will sound more natural.

Vowels before [r] are shown with the symbol [¨] to call attention to the special quality that vowels have before [r]. (Note that the symbols [ä] and [ö] are also used for vowels not followed by [r], as in *box* or *claw*.) You should listen carefully to native speakers to discover how these vowels actually sound.

Stress

This index follows the system for marking stress used in many dictionaries for native speakers.

1. Stress is not marked if a word consisting of a single syllable occurs by itself.

2. Where stress is marked, two levels are distinguished:

a bold accent [/] is placed after each syllable with primary (or strong) stress, a light accent [/] is placed after each syllable with secondary (or weaker) stress. In phrases and other combinations of words, stress is indicated for each word as it would be pronounced within the whole phrase.

Syllable Boundaries

Syllable boundaries are indicated by a single space or by a stress mark.

Note: The pronunciations shown in this index are based on patterns of American English. There has been no attempt to represent all of the varieties of American English. Students should listen to native speakers to hear how the language actually sounds in a particular region.

Index

Index

Index

Index

Index

Index

Index

Index

Index

Index

Index

Index

279

Index

Geographical Index

Geographical Index

Research Bibliography

The authors and publisher wish to acknowledge the contribution of the following educators for their research on vocabulary development, which has helped inform the principals underlying OPD.

Burt, M., J. K. Peyton, and R. Adams. *Reading and Adult English Language Learners: A Review of the Research.* Washington, D.C.: Center for Applied Linguistics, 2003.

Coady, J. "Research on ESL/EFL Vocabulary Acquisition: Putting it in Context." In *Second Language Reading and Vocabulary Learning*, edited by T. Huckin, M. Haynes, and J. Coady. Norwood, NJ: Ablex, 1993.

de la Fuente, M. J. "Negotiation and Oral Acquisition of L2 Vocabulary: The Roles of Input and Output in the Receptive and Productive Acquisition of Words." *Studies in Second Language Acquisition* 24 (2002): 81–112.

DeCarrico, J. "Vocabulary learning and teaching." In *Teaching English as a Second or Foreign Language,* edited by M. Celcia-Murcia. 3rd ed. Boston: Heinle & Heinle, 2001.

Ellis, R. *The Study of Second Language Acquisition.* Oxford: Oxford University Press, 1994.

Folse, K. *Vocabulary Myths: Applying Second Language Research to Classroom Teaching.* Ann Arbor, MI: University of Michigan Press, 2004.

Gairns, R. and S. Redman. *Working with Words: A Guide to Teaching and Learning Vocabulary.* Cambridge: Cambridge University Press, 1986.

Gass, S. M. and M.J.A. Torres. "Attention When?: An Investigation Of The Ordering Effect Of Input And Interaction." *Studies in Second Language Acquisition* 27 (Mar 2005): 1–31.

Henriksen, Birgit. "Three Dimensions of Vocabulary Development." *Studies in Second Language Acquisition* 21 (1999): 303–317.

Koprowski, Mark. "Investigating the Usefulness of Lexical Phrases in Contemporary Coursebooks." *Oxford ELT Journal* 59(4) (2005): 322–32.

McCrostie, James. "Examining Learner Vocabulary Notebooks." *Oxford ELT Journal* 61 (July 2007): 246–55.

Nation, P. *Learning Vocabulary in Another Language.* Cambridge: Cambridge University Press, 2001.

National Center for ESL Literacy Education Staff. *Adult English Language Instruction in the 21st Century.* Washington, D.C.: Center for Applied Linguistics, 2003.

National Reading Panel. *Teaching Children to Read: An Evidenced-Based Assessment of the Scientific Research Literature on Reading and its Implications on Reading Instruction.* 2000. http://www.nationalreadingpanel.org/Publications/summary.htm/.

Newton, J. "Options for Vocabulary Learning Through Communication Tasks." *Oxford ELT Journal* 55(1) (2001): 30–37.

Prince, P. "Second Language Vocabulary Learning: The Role of Context Versus Translations as a Function of Proficiency." *Modern Language Journal* 80(4) (1996): 478-93.

Savage, K. L., ed. *Teacher Training Through Video - ESL Techniques: Early Production.* White Plains, NY: Longman Publishing Group, 1992.

Schmitt, N. *Vocabulary in Language Teaching.* Cambridge: Cambridge University Press, 2000.

Smith, C. B. *Vocabulary Instruction and Reading Comprehension.* Bloomington, IN: ERIC Clearinghouse on Reading English and Communication, 1997.

Wood, K. and J. Josefina Tinajero. "Using Pictures to Teach Content to Second Language Learners." *Middle School Journal* 33 (2002): 47–51.